Population Geography

SECOND EDITION

by

JOHN I. CLARKE

Professor of Geography in the University of Durham

PERGAMON PRESS

OXFORD · NEW YORK · TORONTO · SYDNEY

PARIS · FRANKFURT

U.K.	Pergamon Press Ltd., Headington Hill Hall, Oxford OX3 0BW, England
U.S.A.	Pergamon Press Inc., Maxwell House, Fairview Park, Elmsford, New York 10523, U.S.A.
CANADA	Pergamon of Canada Ltd., 75 The East Mall, Toronto, Ontario, Canada
AUSTRALIA	Pergamon Press (Aust.) Pty. Ltd., 19a Boundary Street, Rushcutters Bay, N.S.W. 2011, Australia
FRANCE	Pergamon Press SARL, 24 rue des Ecoles, 75240 Paris, Cedex 05, France
FEDERAL REPUBLIC OF GERMANY	Pergamon Press GmbH, 6242 Kronberg-Taunus, Pferdstrasse 1, Federal Republic of Germany

First edition 1965
Reprinted 1966
Reprinted with corrections 1968
Reprinted 1969, 1970
Second edition 1972
Reprinted 1974, 1975, 1976 (twice), 1977

Library of Congress Catalog Card No. 70-183339

Printed in Great Britain by A. Wheaton & Co., Exeter
ISBN 0-08-016854 X (flexi cover)
ISBN 0-08-016853 1 (hard cover)

PERGAMON INTERNATIONAL LIBRARY
of Science, Technology, Engineering and Social Studies
The 1000-volume original paperback library in aid of education,
industrial training and the enjoyment of leisure
Publisher: Robert Maxwell, M.C.

Population Geography

PERGAMON OXFORD GEOGRAPHIES

General Editor: W. B. FISHER

Other titles in this series

J. I. CLARKE: Population Geography and the Developing Countries

H. D. CLOUT: The Geography of Post-war France: A Social and Economic Approach

H. D. CLOUT: Rural Geography: An Introductory Survey

R. COOKE & J. H. JOHNSON: Trends in Geography: An Introductory Survey

J. C. A. DEWDNEY: A Geography of the Soviet Union, 2nd Edition

D. W. GILCHRIST SHIRLAW: An Agricultural Geography of Great Britain, 2nd Revised Impression

J. H. JOHNSON: Urban Geography, 2nd Edition

I. G. McINTOSH & C. B. MARSHALL: The Face of Scotland, 2nd Edition

A. M. O'CONNOR: The Geography of Tropical African Development

E. SUNDERLAND: Elements of Human and Social Geography: Some Anthropological Perspectives

The terms of our inspection copy service apply to all the above books. A complete catalogue of all books in the Pergamon International Library is available on request.

CONTENTS

LIST OF ILLUSTRATIONS

PREFACE TO SECOND EDITION

IN THIS extensively revised and extended second edition I am indebted to critics who have urged less brevity than in the first edition, and to research students (particularly Mr. C. A. Palmer) who have made suggestions for specific additions. I must also thank Mrs. P. Blair for retyping much of the text.

Durham   JOHN I. CLARKE

PREFACE TO FIRST EDITION

POPULATION geography is a fairly new aspect of geography. Although geographers have long been interested in the relationships between population distribution and environment, it is only recently that they have considered it necessary to know more about age and sex-structure, migrations and the factors influencing population growth. So they have come into contact with demography, the study of population *per se,* and have studied some of its methods. But the geographical approach is essentially towards the analysis of areal patterns of population distribution, composition, migrations and growth, as well as their causes and consequences upon the cultural landscape.

This volume is systematic, and deals with topics rather than regions, though much of the growing literature is of regional studies. The aim is to introduce young geographers to population study, to explain the geographical approach, and to suggest a frame on which to hang regional studies of population. The book is intended as an introduction to population study for geographers. It is hoped to remedy the paucity of examples and illustrations in a later volume of regional population studies.

Despite several comparable volumes in other languages, no other book in English has been exclusively devoted to this subject. This volume is therefore tentative. It arises from part of an honours degree course given in the University of Durham, in collaboration with Mr. J. C. Dewdney, who considered regional aspects. I owe a debt of gratitude to Professor W. B. Fisher for his encouragements and counsels, and to my wife for her forbearance. I am also grateful to Mr. D. J. Siddle and Mr. K. Swindell for kindly reading the text.

Freetown   JOHN I. CLARKE

CHAPTER I

WHAT IS POPULATION GEOGRAPHY?

Man in Geography

Like the definition of geography, the place of man in geography has long been a matter of academic dispute. Among the earlier geographers attention was largely devoted to the natural environment, although this was considered meaningful only in relation to man. In recent decades there has been progressive reorientation of viewpoint, with increasing emphasis upon man as the main inhabitant of the earth. This approach found its greatest advocates in France, where in the first half of the century a flourishing school of human geography examined and sought to explain the multiple relationships between man, his activities and the environment. However, the views of, for instance, Vidal de la Blache, Jean Brunhes and Maximilien Sorre varied in detail, giving different weight to the study of man. Not surprisingly, human geographers have made many valuable contributions to the study of population distributions. But human geography has not received universal acceptance. Some geographers have considered human geography too broad in scope, englobing as it does the geographical study of economies, societies, settlement, transport and political units. Some have felt that there is little distinction between the terms geography and human geography.

The case for population geography has been most lucidly stated in 1953 by Trewartha, who argued for a focus on man and provided a framework for geographical studies of population. His view is that "numbers, densities, and qualities of the population provide the essential background for all geography. Population is the point of reference from which all other elements are observed, and from which they all, singly and collectively, derive significance and meaning". It must be admitted that such a view would not be endorsed by all geographers, especially those with physical leanings, but there is a growing body whose research and interests are orientated in this way.

Hooson has taken the progressive change in viewpoint to its logical extreme, and postulates that in essence geography is concerned with the problem of the uneven distribution of population over the earth. Distribution of population "acts as a master-thread, capable of weaving into a coherent pattern the otherwise disparate strands of the subject and expressing its philosophical unity, particularly in the context of regional geography". He emphasizes the importance of examining the ideas of men about place, rather than objective studies of place itself. Hooson considers that there is no need for a distinct sub-division of geography called population geography, which in his view would be in danger of becoming the whole of geography.

Whilst there are many who will be sympathetic to this view of geography, and agree that studies of population distribution provide a spine for regional geography, and a theme for geography as a whole, many will regard it as too narrow or too anthropocentric. In any case, population geography has evolved as a distinct branch of geography — not before time, some will confess, in the light of the numerous other specialist branches of the subject. Indeed, the wonder is that its evolution has been so slow, when we consider the growing awareness of the significance of population growth in social and economic development.

Population Geography and Demography

Population geography, or geography of population — the terms have the same meaning — is concerned with demonstrating how spatial variations in the distribution, composition, migrations and growth of populations are related to spatial variations in the nature of places. The population geographer is also concerned with the genetic or dynamic aspects of spatial variations over time, or how spatial relations or interaction between phenomena occur. The emphasis is particularly on space, and in this way population geography distinguishes itself from demography, which is the science of population viewed as a single topic. In practice, while the demographer is concerned with numbers and demographic processes especially for political units as wholes, the population geographer is more concerned with areal variations in population and their relations with physical, cultural and economic phenomena.

Like demography, population geography is basically quantitative; it is largely dependent upon statistical data. But both have a qualitative approach; demographers examine various physical, intellectual and character qualities of populations to see their connections with quantitative aspects, while population geographers endeavour to unravel the complex inter-relationships between physical and human environments on the one hand, and population on the other. The explanation and analysis of these inter-relationships is the real substance of population geography.

Knowledge of the elementary techniques of demography is indispensable to the population geographer. They are basic tools, the ignorance of which may result in false correlations or incomplete analysis. Dependence upon a neighbouring science is not an unusual attribute of branches of systematic or topical geography. It is a natural consequence of geography's character as a correlative subject. Just as economic geographers, biogeographers and geomorphologists require basic training in economics, biology and geology, so population geographers must be aware of the methods of demography. Therefore this volume devotes much space to simple demographic techniques.

Eastern and Western Views of Population Geography

In recent years a spate of papers on population geography has appeared in geographical journals and edited symposia. In Western countries the evolution and organization of the subject owes much to the pleas of Trewartha, the stimulus of the International Geographic Union, the pioneer systematic and regional studies of the French geographers George and Beaujeu-Garnier, and the propagandist zeal of Zelinsky. But although Zelinsky argues that "we have every right to expect that population geography will shift from its present, rather peripheral standing to a commanding position within the discipline", like many others he finds some difficulty in circumscribing the field of population geography. He concludes that the list of human characteristics of practical interest to the population geographer may be equated with "those appearing in the census enumeration schedules and vital registration systems of the more statistically advanced nations". The human characteristics fall into three groups:

   (a) absolute numbers;
   (b) (i) physical characteristics: age, sex, race, morbidity, intelligence;
       (ii) social characteristics: marital status, family, household, residence, literacy, education, language, religion, nationality, ethnic group;
       (iii) economic characteristics: industry, occupation, income;
   (c) population dynamics: fertility, mortality, migration, change.

This range of human characteristics is not enumerated by all advanced countries, but as a field of study it would gain considerable acceptance from population geographers in Western countries, and it forms the basis of this short volume. Unfortunately, however, it is not possible to do justice to all these aspects of population; some will receive more treatment than others, partly because they are more central to the theme of population geography and partly because they have attracted closer attention from geographers.

This Western view of population geography would not gain widespread acceptance in the Soviet Union. Orthodox Marxist geographers have rejected human geography because of its early association with crude geographic determinism and its emphasis on the relationships between the individual and the environment. The basic tenets of Marxist theory lie counter to the view that man could be moulded, consciously or unconsciously, by his physical environment. To Marxists, man and his social organization are the measure and dominating factors of human existence. They also consider that the productive aspects of population are the most important in the distribution of population, and consequently regard population geography as within the framework of economic geography. Their conception of population geography is much wider than in the West; it also includes the geography of towns and rural settlements, historical geography of population, ethnographic geography and the geography of labour resources. With the exception of the last, this list reads like the components of many Western courses in human or social geography. Melezin describes Soviet geography of population as "the study of population distribution and productive relationships existing within various population groups, the settlement network and its fitness, usefulness, and effectiveness for productive goals of a society", although a variety of Soviet definitions exist, as seen in the October 1967 issue of *Soviet Geography*. Special attention has been devoted to urban geography and the geography of rural settlements, because population distribution is now represented by a network of settlements which is affected by changes in social production. In particular, attempts have been made to elucidate the general principles underlying population geography, such as those postulated by Pokshishevskii and summarized by Melezin as follows:

"1. The type of economy determines the character of settlement and its forms.

2. Distribution and territorial organization of production decides all manifestations of natural conditions and their influence upon settlement and its forms.

3. Adaptability of migrants to a new geographic environment is influenced by already existing work habits and skills. This factor loses its importance with higher development of productive forces.

4. The complexity of industry and the magnitude of performed functions by cities and towns determine their population size.

5. The economic-geographic situation of towns influences the concentration and types of functions performed by them."

In the U.S.S.R. population geography has advanced in recent years to become one of the major research fields in economic geography, and has acquired a practical role in planned organization and development. There can be no doubt that population geography has universal utility in regional and urban planning. Nowhere is there greater need for studies of population geography than in the newly emergent, statistically backward and developing countries which are striving to elevate their standards of living.

Analysis of population is also an essential element of all regional geography, although past regional studies have too often involved detailed examinations of environment, habitat and economy and neglected the manifold demographic influences and effects. Without serious consideration of such aspects it is impossible to assess the social and economic evolution of any region.

Human Populations

In this book we are interested only in human populations, although the term "population" is commonly used with reference to all other members of the plant and animal kingdoms. It may also be noted that in statistics "population" has an even wider meaning.

Human populations differ from animal populations in several important ways. Among vertebrates we are a numerous species, and because of our large body size we probably outweigh in sheer overall bulk as a group any other species. We are outnumbered, however, by codfish, sardines and grasshoppers, but are unique in being aware of our population as a problem. Fertility and mortality of human populations are less fluctuating than among animals, and the evolutionary character of the human race is more stable. Human fertility is low because of the short reproductive period, natural and artificial fertility checks, cultural restraints as well as increasing numbers in the post-reproductive age-groups. Human mortality is also unusual in that it results largely from old age and disease — rare occurrences among animals, who suffer more from predation and food shortages associated with high densities. The latter have no significant direct effect upon human mortality, although urban congestion certainly affects our health. Another significant aspect of human populations vis-à-vis animal populations is our impact upon animals, whose numbers and environments in many parts of the world have been greatly transformed. This is a reflection of the ubiquity and mobility of man.

References

On population geography see:

BEAUJEU-GARNIER, J., *Géographie de la population*, 2 vols., 1956–7.
BEAUJEU-GARNIER, J., *Geography of Population*, 1966.
DEMKO, G. J., ROSE, H. M. and SCHNELL, G. A., *Population Geography: A Reader*, 1970.
GEORGE, P., *Introduction à l'étude géographique de la population du monde*, 1951.
GEORGE, P., *Questions de géographie de la population*, 1959.
GEORGE, P., *Géographie de la population*, 1965.
HOOSON, D. J. M., The distribution of population as the essential geographical expression, *Canadian Geographer*, **17**, 10 (1960).
JAMES, P. E., The geographic study of population, in JAMES, P. E. and JONES, C. F. (Eds.), *American Geography: Inventory and Prospect*, 106 (1954).
MELEZIN, A., Trends and issues in the Soviet geography of population, *Ann. Assoc. Amer. Geographers*, **53**, 144 (1963).
POKSHISHEVSKII, V. V., Geography of population and its tasks, *Soviet Geography: Review and Translation*, **3**, 9 (1962).
SORRE, M., *Les Fondements de la géographie humaine*, 4 vols., 1943–52.

Soviet Geography: Review and Translation, **8** (Oct. 1967).
TREWARTHA, G. T., The case for population geography, *Ann. Assoc. Amer. Geographers*, **43**, 71 (1953).
TREWARTHA, G. T., *A Geography of Population: World Patterns*, 1969.
WILSON, M. G. A., *Population Geography*, 1968.
ZELINSKY, W., *A Bibliographic Guide to Population Geography*, Univ. of Chicago Dept. of Geography Research Paper 20 (1962).
ZELINSKY, W., *A Prologue to Population Geography*, 1965.

For the principles and problems of demography see:

BENJAMIN, B., *Demographic Analysis*, 1968.
BOGUE, D., *Principles of Demography*, New York, 1969.
COX, P. R., *Demography*, 1961.
HAUSER, P. M. and DUNCAN, O. D., *The Study of Population: An Inventory and Appraisal*, 1959.
PETERSEN, W., *Population*, New York, 2nd ed., 1969.
LYNN SMITH, T., *Fundamentals of Population Study*, Chicago, 1960.
SPENGLER, J. J. and DUNCAN, O. D. (Eds.), *Demographic Analysis: Selected Readings*, Glencoe, Ill., 1956.
THOMLINSON, R., *Population Dynamics: Causes and Consequences of World Demographic Change*, New York, 1965.
THOMPSON, W. S. and LEWIS, D. T., *Population Problems*, New York, 5th ed., 1965.
U.N. Population Studies No. 17, *The Determinants and Consequences of Population Trends*, 1953.
VILLEY, D., *Leçons de démographie*, 2 vols., 1957–8.

See also the four journals *Population Index*, Princeton; *Population Studies*, Cambridge; *Population*, Paris; and *Demography*, Chicago.
The U.N. *Demographic Yearbooks* are indispensable.

CHAPTER II

TYPES AND PROBLEMS OF DATA

Quality of Data

Among the most difficult problems of the population geographer are that population data vary in character and quality in time and space. In general, the more advanced countries and regions have more accurate and more profuse population statistics than the backward countries and regions, although strenuous efforts have been made in recent years, especially by the United Nations Organization, to assist backward countries by arranging censuses and statistical services.

International population data suffer from inaccuracy and heterogeneity. Inaccuracy results from (a) poor and inadequately financed methods of collection; (b) suspicion, resentment and ignorance of censuses; (c) false statements, especially of age and occupation; (d) constant changes in population; and (e) omissions of more inaccessible areas and some population groups. Heterogeneity results from (a) diversity in types and comprehensiveness of enumeration; (b) lack of synchronization of national censuses; (c) frequent changes in boundaries of political, administrative and census units; (d) wide differences in connotation of terms like language, household, race, nationality, occupation, urban population, still-birth, etc. Again, through their numerous demographic publications, the United Nations Organization has endeavoured to evaluate demographic data and to bring some measure of uniformity by recommendations as to periodicity of censuses, types of questions, and definition of terms. During recent decades many countries have held their first national census under the efficient auspices of UNO.

Types of Population Data

Broadly speaking, students of population are interested in two main aspects: (a) the state of the population at any given time, including its geographic distribution and its structure or composition; and (b) the movement or dynamics of population in time and space, i.e. its growth or decline by the actions of fertility, mortality and migrations.

Furthermore, there are two groups of methods of obtaining data: (a) static methods for ascertaining distribution and structure (censuses, sample surveys,

7

population commissions and enquiries); and (b) dynamic methods for measuring (i) population movement (vital registration of births, marriages and deaths, as well as migration records), and (ii) changes in population structure (records of change in occupation, employment, etc.). The former methods have been compared with a photograph, an instantaneous record; the latter, like a film, are a continuous record.

The Census

Although enumerations of population were carried out in ancient times, the earliest modern censuses of countries took place in Scandinavia and some Germanic and Italian States during the eighteenth century. The first and very imperfect general census of the United States occurred in 1790, although there had been earlier state censuses. In 1801 Britain and France held their first censuses, and subsequently throughout the nineteenth century all European countries initiated periodic population censuses. During this century, especially since the Second World War, the census has extended to most countries of the world, although even as late as 1968 there were a number of countries yet to hold a census: Afghanistan, Bhutan, Ethiopia, Laos, Lebanon, Somali Republic, South Vietnam, Southern Yemen and Yemen.

A census has been defined as "the total process of collecting, compiling and publishing demographic data pertaining, at a particular time, to all persons in a defined territory". Periodicity is an important characteristic of censuses. So also is universality, the need to include every individual in a given area or, if sampling is used, the need to give every member of a stratum the same likelihood of inclusion. But the concept of censuses differs. By the *de facto* approach, used in Great Britain, each individual is recorded at the place where he was found at the time of the census. By the *de jure* approach, used in the United States, people are recorded according to their usual residence. In Brazil, both approaches are used. Unfortunately, population mobility, the multiple residences of some and the homelessness of others make the *de jure* approach less satisfactory than the *de facto* method, although the *de facto* enumeration may give enlarged totals to holiday resorts.

There is a wide variety in the types and quantity of data covered by the different national censuses. One country includes only 12 types of data; some include 24. Most censuses include geographic location, age, sex, marital status, citizenship, place of birth, relationship to the head of household, religion, educational characteristics, and economic characteristics of occupation, industry and status. Much less common are census data of fertility, nuptiality, secondary occupation, income, language, ethnic characteristics, native customs, disabilities and migration.

The United Nations recommend that the census should determine the following: (a) total population; (b) sex, age and marital status; (c) place of birth, citizenship or nationality; (d) mother tongue, literacy and educational qualifications; (e) economic characteristics; (f) urban or rural domicile; (g) household or family structure; and (h) fertility. It is a tall order, which in some countries can only be satisfactorily fulfilled by sampling techniques.

Census data are not always useful to the geographer. Apart from problems of inaccuracy, inadequacy and delay in publication, census data may be reduced in value to geographers by the unsuitability of classifications used and the difficulty of retrieving the original figures.

Vital Registration

The census method of collecting birth and death data is not satisfactory because it is not a continuous process and because reports by respondents to questionnaires are inaccurate as to dates. Far more satisfactory is vital registration, which is the continuous, compulsory and legal recording of vital events, like births, deaths, marriages, divorces, annulments, separations and adoptions.

Although parish registers and "Bills of Mortality" assist us in ascertaining information about population growth in pre-Victorian England, the first central form of vital registration occurred in 1836. Through the efforts of Dr. William Farr it was made compulsory in 1874. His system of vital statistics in England and Wales was the example for modern systems elsewhere, but we should realize that its development has been slow; still-births in this country were not registered until 1926. While Scandinavian records of vital registration are much older than those of Britain, and adequate data are available for advanced countries, many areas of the world do not have even the most rudimentary data. Crude birth and death rates are not available for nearly half of the world's population, while marriage and divorce statistics are available for no more than one-third.

On the whole, vital registration data tend to be more precise than those of censuses, except information about causes of death and ages of women. But again the amount and type of information varies greatly between countries. In some countries over 50 different items of information may occur on the statistical report forms of births, deaths, marriages and divorces; in others as few as 4. In the former case analytical possibilities are almost unlimited; in the latter there are great blanks in our knowledge. In birth statistics, for example, we often have no record of the religion of the parents, or their citizenship, occupation, industry, race, literacy and language.

Sample Surveys

The value of sampling in the collection of population data is well known. Costs can be greatly reduced without substantial reductions in accuracy.

Sample surveys are increasingly used for national enumerations, particularly in the former French possessions in Africa, where for political reasons a complete census may give less reliable results. Moreover, sampling may also be used within censuses, as in Britain, in order to obtain more detailed information, although the 1966 census was entirely on a 10 per cent household basis. Sampling may also be used to supplement census data; in the United States a continuous representative sampling technique is operated. The country is divided into 68 fairly homogeneous regions termed "strata", which are then subdivided into fairly heterogeneous "primary sampling units" of which one is chosen from each stratum. Then typical "areas" are selected from each unit according to needs, and in these areas a complete list of dwellings is compiled and a quasi-random sample obtained.

Migration Records

The quality of data on migration is usually much poorer than that on the composition and growth of population. The reasons are varied. Migrations occur in multiple forms, not easily defined or classified. Classifications based on the duration of migration, distance covered or organization (e.g. spontaneous, forced or state organized) are only arbitrary. Migrants can also be extremely difficult to enumerate, especially where they do not cross any significant administrative boundary.

In the past much of the information on internal migrations has been obtained from comparison of successive census enumerations after allowance had been made for natural increase. Now some censuses request information on change of residence and place of birth which facilitates migration analysis, though birthplace data give only a crude indication of population movement. Comparison of data of usual residence and workplace — available for the 1921 and 1951 censuses (and a 10 per cent sample of the 1961 census) of England and Wales — enables study of journey to work. In the 1961 census of England and Wales a new question was included to obtain information about the volume, frequency, direction and characteristics of internal migrations. In general, however, internal migration data remain among the least accurate of all demographic data.

Statistics of international migrations are available for only a small minority of countries. Moreover, they are notoriously unreliable and have low comparability. Each country collects only the data which it needs for its own administrative purposes. Data are drawn from a variety of sources: frontier control, port statistics, passport statistics of certain categories of travellers, local population registers, work permits for aliens, etc. The common categories of long-term (permanent) migrant, short-term (temporary) migrant, visitor and resident used in U.N. publications are purely conventional, for even legal definitions vary greatly, and definitions are based on intentions. In 1953 the United Nations made numerous recommendations which have helped to clarify the issues, but it must be remembered that many international migrants still escape enumeration, especially where frontiers are long, geometric, bisect human groups or are poorly controlled.

Other Sources of Data

Only the primary sources of population data have been mentioned. In Britain we have available the *Registrar-General's Quarterly Returns*, the *Reports of the Ministry of Health*, the *Ministry of Labour's Register of Disabled Persons*, the *Census of Production*, the *Census of Distribution*, the *Monthly Digest of Statistics*, Friendly Society records, electoral registers (which have been used for detailed urban population studies), and many other sources. Other countries are not so fortunate in this respect.

The United Nations Statistical Office, the World Health Organization and the International Labour Office act as central agencies for much national data and assist in increasing its comparability.

Areal Units

The population geographer is particularly dependent upon the areal units for which enumerations have been made. There are three types: (a) administrative units; (b) combinations of administrative units, which are not political entities themselves; (c) special units devised for statistical purposes. In many cases the geographer is concerned less with such units than with areas characterized by internal homogeneity or nodality. Such areas are rarely coincident, as nodal regions are characterized more by diversity than by homogeneity, and nodal centres often occur at or near boundaries of discontinuities in homogeneity. Exemplifying this problem is the case of a student faced with a regional dissertation and trying to decide whether to select natural boundaries or administrative ones. Many students succumb to the attractions of the latter, because of the greater ease of statistical analysis, though they may have little geographical significance.

Above all, geographers should consider areal units as areas, not as units. The tabulation of population numbers by country or by county is not meaningful geographically unless consideration is given to internal distribution. But the arbitrariness of metropolitan and municipal boroughs, of urban and rural districts, and of parishes impedes our tasks. Recourse to the smallest areal units, the enumeration districts or census tracts, often is the only source of satisfaction to the population geographer. Many of these units are sufficiently homogeneous to enable greater dependence upon their boundaries.

Revisions of boundaries of census units are the bugbear of the population geographer anxious to map intercensal population changes. In Britain boundary revisions are extremely common, and simple comparisons of areal data over many decades are often invalidated.

Dissatisfaction with the areal units for which census data are provided has led to many analyses using grid mashes, and also to the proposal by Robertson that "maximum flexibility in the presentation of data and in the units of area to which they refer could be achieved by (a) allocating to every individual and every dwelling a unique locational reference, such as a twelve-figure National Grid reference; (b) storing the coded records of individuals and dwellings as a census data bank". Certainly this would facilitate the application of mathematics to population geography. The geocoding system implemented in the 1971 British census was a great advance, as for most of the country households were referenced to 100 m. squares and for a selection of areas covered by 1:1250 maps full co-ordinate referencing was undertaken for residential premises.

Finally, it may be noted that the size of areal units studied has a real relevance to population dynamics, particularly the relative significance of migrations and natural increase, for while at the world level migration as yet plays no part in population change and at the continental level its role is subordinate to natural increase, at the national level its role is often much greater, especially in small states, and at the local level it may be the main element of population change. In a world so politically divided, the size of a state may therefore greatly influence its population dynamics, and consequently small States (e.g. Hong Kong, Kuwait, Israel) and islands are more demographically unstable than large States (e.g. China, India). One result of this is that there is a problem in linking results obtained at one scale to those obtained at another.

References

BARCLAY, G. W., *Techniques of Population Analysis*, New York, 1958.
BENJAMIN, B., *Demographic Analysis*, 1968.
BENJAMIN, B., *The Population Census*, 1970.
FORBES, J. and ROBERTSON, I. M. L., Population enumeration on a grid square basis: the census of Scotland, a test case, *Cartographic Journal*, **4**, 29 (1967).
KEYFITZ, N., *Introduction to the Mathematics of Population*, Reading, Mass., 1968.
KEYFITZ, N. and FLIEGER, W., *World Population: An Analysis of Vital Data*, Chicago, 1968.
MEDVEDKOV, V. V., Applications of mathematics to population geography, *Soviet Geography: Review and Translation*, **8**, 709 (1967).
ROBERTSON, I. M. L., The census and research: ideals and realities, *Trans. and Papers Inst. Brit. Geographers*, **48**, 173 (1969).
U.N. *Handbook of Vital Statistics Methods*, 1955.
U.N. *Handbook of Population Census Methods*, 3 vols., 1965.
YATES, F., *Sampling Methods for Censuses and Surveys*, 1959.

CHAPTER III

WORLD DISTRIBUTION OF POPULATION

Diversity of Distribution

In 1969 the world's population amounted to about 3552 millions, inhabiting more than 136 million square kilometres of land. The distribution by continents is most uneven:

	Number (millions)	Density (per sq. km.)	Percentage of world population
Africa	345	11	9·6
North America	224	10	6·4
Latin America	276	13	7·7
Asia	1988	72	55·9
Oceania	19	2	0·5
Europe (without U.S.S.R.)	460	93	13·1
U.S.S.R.	240	11	6·8
	3552	26	100·0

The Old World is far more populous than the New. Europe and Asia together contain well over three-quarters of mankind; Asia, with or without the U.S.S.R., has more than half, and Europe alone has more than either the New World or the three southern continents. The Americas sustain only 14·1 per cent of the total population, and the three southern continents only 15·3 per cent.

The distribution by latitudes is just as varied. Less than 10 per cent of the world's population live in the southern hemisphere, just over 10 per cent between the equator and 20°N, nearly 50 per cent between 20°N and 40°N, 30 per cent between 40°N and 60°N, and less than one-half per cent north of 60°N. In other words, nearly four-fifths of mankind live between 20°N and 60°N, mainly in the Old World. Yet this zone includes most of the great deserts of the northern hemisphere as wel as the Alpine–Himalayan mountain chains. It also contains the bulk of the four major concentrations of humanity

13

(in South and East Asia, Europe and the north-eastern part of North America), where about 63 per cent of the world's population live on 10 per cent of the world's land area (see Fig. 1).

The secondary concentrations are both more numerous and more scattered: California, coastal Brazil, the Plate estuary, the Nile valley, West Africa, south-east Australia. But the blanks on the world population map are much larger than areas of high density; some 64 per cent of the land area has densities less than 2 per sq. km and 35–40 per cent may be regarded as uninhabited.

Disparity in population size and density is also striking at the national level. In Asia (excluding the U.S.S.R.) there are five states with about 100 million inhabitants or more — the Chinese Republic, India, Pakistan, Japan and Indonesia — incorporating nearly half of the world's population. In contrast, the 100 million people of West Africa are located in fifteen political divisions. Indeed, in the African continent there are many political divisions with less than a million inhabitants: Swaziland, Lesotho, Botswana, Cabinda, Gambia, Gabon, Congo (Brazzaville), Djibouti, Portuguese Guinea, Equatorial Guinea, Spanish Sahara and South-West Africa. Europe, too, has its pocket populations: Liechtenstein, Monaco, Iceland, Luxembourg, Andorra, and the Vatican City.

The diversity of world population distribution cannot be examined here in detail. The variety of distributions is so great that there can be no adequate simple classification of types. Between a regular dispersed pattern and an uneven nuclear pattern there is a whole gamut of population distributions, responding to a wide range of changing environmental and human influences. Even the most densely peopled regions can contain uninhabited forests, heaths or parks; even very sparsely populated regions may contain oases, mining camps or research stations.

Influences upon Population Distribution

We cannot subscribe to the purely deterministic viewpoint which holds that natural elements are the controlling factors of population distribution. Physical factors alone will not explain population distribution whether it be in Africa, Argentina, Arkansas or Adelaide; their influence is greater in some places than in others, but everywhere man exercises some control over his habitat. Numerous social, demographic, economic, political and historical factors must be considered, not in isolation, but as interrelated influences upon population distribution. The geographer's task is to explain the diversity of this distribution in terms of all these influences, not merely for a given moment in time, but as an integral part of a dynamic process. Population distribution is ever changing, and cause and effect vary in time and space.

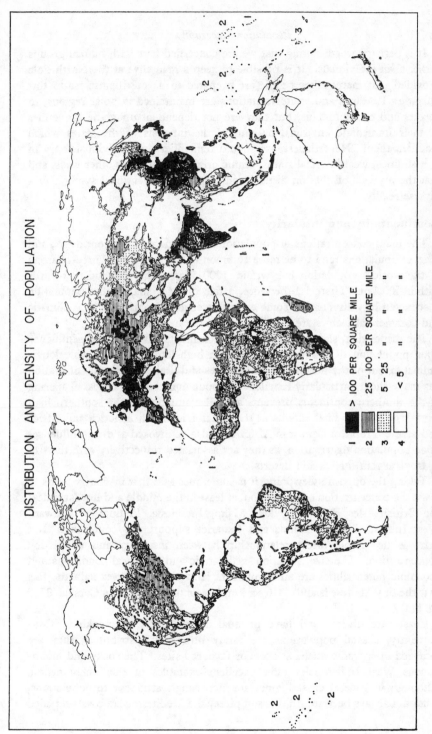

DISTRIBUTION AND DENSITY OF POPULATION

1	> 100 PER SQUARE MILE
2	25 - 100 PER SQUARE MILE
3	5 - 25 " " "
4	< 5 " " "

FIG. 1. The world distribution and density of population. Simplified from *The Times Atlas of the World*, Vol. 1, 1958.

It is perhaps worth noting that we are concerned here with human groups rather than individuals. It is possible to keep a man alive at the North Pole provided that many other people are prepared to devote themselves to this purpose. Research and strategic stations are maintained in polar regions, in deserts and on mountains, but they are not dependent upon the economies of their immediate environs, only upon the interests of the states which maintain them. Nevertheless, we should remember that individuals vary in age, abilities, wealth, social status, ethnic origin and in many other ways, and that the myriads of dots on distribution maps are conventional symbols of a diverse reality.

Continentality and Insularity

The main concentrations of population are marginal to the continents, and sparse populations tend to be more common in the interiors. Three-quarters of the world's population live within 1000 km of the sea, and two-thirds within 500 km. There is, therefore, a fair case for stating that population is attracted by coasts and to some extent repelled by continentality. Climatic and commercial factors are the main influences here involved.

The disposition, shape and size of the continents have a primary influence upon population distribution, especially in high latitudes. The wide longitudinal extent of the northern high latitudes and limited maritime infiltration has made them particularly repellent to population concentrations. Tapering of the southern continents prevents a similar situation in the southern high latitudes. Longitudinal extents at the equator in South America and Africa and at the Tropic of Cancer in Africa may also be invoked as direct influences upon population distribution, as they are associated respectively with the size of tropical rain forests and deserts.

Taking the opposite viewpoint, it is sometimes said that insularity tends to assist the concentration of population, at least in the middle and low latitudes: the British Isles, Japan, Ceylon, Malta, Indonesia, Philippines, Taiwan, West Indies, Channel Islands and Canaries support this contention. But there is no simple direct relationship between insularity and population concentration. The size, situation, geographic and historical conditions and economic potentialities are all significant. How else can one explain the fact that the tiny Maltese islands (316 sq. km) have more people than Corsica (8720 sq. km)?

Coasts are diverse and have unequal attractiveness to mankind. Consequently, coastal populations are rarely uniformly distributed; they are localized in sporadic nuclei at ports or favoured sites. The rocky and mountainous West Indian isles offer excellent examples of this phenomenon. Although in general coastal zones are increasingly attractive to populations, it has not always been so. In times of piracy the Mediterranean coasts repelled population. Similarly, the coastal belt of West Africa was depopulated during the height of the slave trade.

The respective influences of continentality and insularity do not operate in isolation; they are associated with other factors, and thus many obvious exceptions spring to mind: the high densities in Rwanda and Burundi, Szechwan and the Moscow Basin and the low densities in Borneo, Tasmania and Iceland.

Vertical Distribution of Population

In an exhaustive world analysis of the vertical distribution of population, Staszewski has shown that population numbers and densities diminish with altitude, a reflection of the increasing difficulties entailed in the exploitation of high geographic environments and adaptation to them. In Fig. 2, graphs depict percentages and densities of the various continental populations at different elevations. Apparently, 56·2 per cent of the world's population live between sea-level and 200 metres above, which includes only 27·8 per cent of the total land area; the density of population at this lowest level is about twice the world average. Just over four-fifths live under 500 metres on 57·3 per cent of land area. Staszewski made similar calculations for all the countries in the world, attempting to discover critical elevations for habitation.

The massive populations of Asia have had a great influence upon the proportions of the world's population at various hypsometric levels; the percentage curves for Asia and the world as a whole are very similar. Britain is atypical; over four-fifths of her population live between 0 and 100 metres above sea-level.

By constructing hypsometric curves of population, Staszewski was able to calculate the mean level of the vertical distribution of population for the various continents:

Africa	590 metres		N. America	430 metres
Asia	319 „		S. America	644 „
Australia	95 „			
Europe	168 „		World	320 „

High altitude alone imposes an ultimate physiological limit upon human habitation, because the drastic reduction in atmospheric pressure and oxygen pressure is dangerous to man. High altitudes require some adaptation, but this enables permanent habitation at altitudes up to 5200 metres in the Andes. Between this height and 6700 metres are critical limits to permanent occupation.

Altitude cannot be dissociated from latitude as a criterion of population distribution. In low latitudes, altitude may be advantageous to human occupation because of climatic amelioration. The relatively high population

densities of the Ethiopian highlands owe much to this influence; Addis Ababa
is in the heart of a rich agricultural region at 2450 metres. Mountains in
Latin America are often much healthier than plains, and cities are often at
high altitudes: La Paz lies at 3640 metres, Quito at 2850, Bogota at 2650 and
Mexico City at 2355. In contrast, the highest town in Britain is Buxton
at 305 metres, for, conversely, high altitude is a disadvantage to habitation in
high latitudes.

VERTICAL DISTRIBUTION OF POPULATION

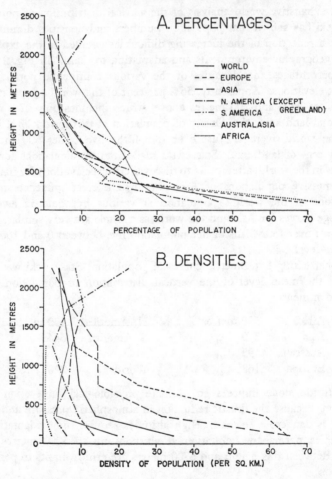

FIG. 2. Vertical distribution of population in the world and the continents.
Diagram A shows the percentage of the total population at various height
intervals, while diagram B shows the density of population at these height
intervals. (After Staszewski.)

Population and Relief

Steep slopes, exposure and ruggedness play their part in restricting human access, habitation and cultivation. It is true that most of these disadvantages can be overcome by technical invention and ingenuity, but in general they are not conducive to dense human settlement. On the other hand, this has not prevented their occupation in regions of overpopulation or insecurity. Often plainsmen have moved into mountains taking with them agricultural techniques which they used on the plains. In the Atlas mountains of North Africa can be found a variety of modes of life ranging from pure nomadism to sedentary cultivation which have frequently originated elsewhere and have been adapted to new environments. Many of the peoples living in these mountains took refuge there in times of stress or danger, and now we find, for example in Kabylie in northern Algeria, densely peopled mountain massifs with resources quite incapable of sustaining the population. Nor are the Atlas mountains unusual in this respect; in the Balkans, Turkey and Iran are many mountain refuge communities.

The mere mass of mountains is a significant factor, especially in middle and high latitudes; the enormity and barrenness of the plateaux of Inner Asia exemplify this. Moreover, sharp transitions between mountain and plain generally mean abrupt changes in population density; one thinks of such diverse examples as the Rockies, the Ochils in Scotland, Dartmoor and Japan.

Valleys are routes of penetration and zones of occupation in mountains, sometimes arteries, sometimes culs-de-sac. Population maps of Highland Scotland or of Tasmania would illustrate this point. Slope and aspect have considerable influence upon the location of population along these valleys where insolation is so important.

Many mountains, in advanced and developing countries alike, are now experiencing considerable depopulation, because of changes in economic structure, security or demographic growth. In temperate zones at least, mountain land is often marginal land agriculturally, and has less commercial value than lowlands. This is an important factor in the problem of the depopulating highlands.

Piedmont areas, zones of contact between different environments, are often areas of dense population: central Scotland, north-east England, the West Riding, Nottingham and Lancashire, although coal is here an additional influence. The loessial belt of northern Europe and the Fall Line towns of the United States are other examples of piedmonts with dense populations. On a smaller scale, spring-line villages are a comparable example of this phenomenon.

Plains are normally more advantageous to human occupancy than mountains, yet many of the world's largest plains are for one reason or another only sparsely populated: the Amazon and Congo basins, the plains of the Sahara, Siberia and the Lake Eyre basin.

The fact is that, while a cursory perusal of a topographic map will reveal that landforms as a whole exert a considerable influence upon population distribution, examination of a variety of maps will demonstrate that particular landforms do not exert a constant influence. Their influence depends upon the whole pattern of relief as well as upon other environmental and human factors, not least of which is man's changing technical ability to use the landforms around him.

The same qualification applies to the influence of rivers. Many attract population through their usefulness as sources of water, fish, fowl, alluvial gold and diamonds, and as media of transport. They also attract by being obstacles to land transport; fords, ferries and bridges have often instigated urban growth. Settlements are often found at the spring-line, at the head of navigation, at a confluence, at the lowest bridging point, where an island occurs in the river, within a loop or bend of a river, where a river forms a gap in hills, where it leaves the hills for the plains, or where it enters a lake.

But rivers are not always attractive to settlement. They may be too infested with mosquitoes or game, too liable to flooding or too deeply incised, too dangerously braided or too torrential, too narrow or too wide. In deserts, rivers are attractive — no ribbon of population rivals the Nile valley — but in tropical swamps and dissected plateaux they may repel population; for example, in northern Ghana onchocerciasis (river blindness) has repelled population from river valleys. There can be no rules, but the geographer cannot afford to neglect the influence (positive or negative) of rivers upon population distribution.

The Influence of Climate

The influence of climate upon population distribution is immensely important, not only directly upon the human organism but also indirectly through its effects upon soils, vegetation and agriculture. Prolonged human habitat, by populations rather than individuals, is only possible within certain limits of temperature, rainfall, humidity, light and electrical charge. Certainly the limitations imposed by climate account for many of the uninhabited and sparsely peopled areas of the earth's surface. Huntington and others carried the argument much further and saw climate as the mainspring of civilizations, the impulse for migrations, the determinant of the energy and character of nations. Deterministic correlations of this magnitude have inspired many opponents, who have stressed man's ability to adapt himself to different climates, an ability which is augmented by technical progress.

Climatic optima are difficult to define in view of the number of climatic variables, the variety of optima for different modes of life and types of work, and man's increasing ability to create suitable micro-climates, e.g. by central heating. In general, while population concentrations do not strictly conform to climatic optima, extremes of climate tend to repel population.

The main exceptions to this generalization are the great population concentrations within the tropics, usually considered far from the climatic optima. The suitability of humid heat for human habitation has been a matter of some dispute; the answer to the enigma of the markedly unequal population concentrations of South-East Asia and the equatorial zones of Africa and South America lies in a complex of environmental and human phenomena, including differing physiological and social adaptation to local conditions. While humid heat is conducive to rapid vegetal growth, permits multiple cropping and reduces requirements for clothing and shelter, it also assists the propagation of plant, animal and human diseases. The adaptation of white populations to these conditions is difficult, and they have found it desirable to make periodic visits to more temperate zones; hence the growth of summer capitals in India. But tropical peoples also find the benefit of such visits. Mediterranean peoples have generally become acclimatized to tropical climates more easily than West Europeans, as in Queensland and Brazil.

Cold climates are much less suitable for human habitation. The northern high latitudes have one-tenth of the total land area, but only a few thousandths of the total population. Eskimoes are considerably adapted by development of subcutaneous tissue and have been successful in protecting themselves by special clothing and dwellings, but the main deterrent to population concentrations has been the cessation of vegetal growth, the absence of fresh vegetables and the prevalence of scurvy. About 16·6 million sq. km of the earth's surface are too cold for crop growth. Other repellents in northern latitudes are the long polar night and the low insolation of summer, which may provoke psychological depression and may adversely affect fertility. Yet there is increasing settlement of these difficult latitudes in the U.S.S.R.

High temperatures alone do not prevent human habitation, but in combination with low and irregular rainfall they drastically diminish habitability. Covering nearly one-fifth of the earth's surface, the deserts contain only one-twenty-fifth of the total population. Life in deserts depends upon water, and so the main nuclei of population occur where water is available — either along rivers whose sources are outside the deserts (e.g. Nile, Indus) or around underground water supplies. However, oases are rarely populous, and nomadic and semi-nomadic pastoralists are never numerous because they rely on meagre pastures. In addition to the arid areas, the semi-arid lands permit only sparse agricultural populations, unless irrigation is developed.

In mining, industrial and scientific centres in both hot and cold climates modern techniques permit solutions to climatic extremes. Compact modern

communities can exist in the middle of the Sahara and in the far north of
Canada and the U.S.S.R., but they survive through external supplies.

Along the margins of the great uninhabited areas population density may
be considerably affected by climatic oscillations. Huntington regarded these
oscillations as "the pulse of Asia", stimulating migrations from the arid heart
of the continent towards the periphery. Along desert fringes periods of
prolonged drought have caused depopulation. The Icelandic peoples through
the ages have also been particularly responsive to climatic changes, not only
in their distribution but even in their stature, which was affected by the
frequency of famine years. Climatic causes of human migrations may sometimes be exaggerated, while social, economic and political reasons are ignored.
Nevertheless, in many parts of the world there is ample evidence of the
significance of climatic vagaries upon the distribution of mankind.

Population and Soils

Like any other factor of the physical environment, soils are difficult to
isolate as an influence upon population distribution, but their influence is
undeniable. The fertile alluvial soils of the deltas of South-East Asia and the
Nile can support dense agricultural populations. So can the chernozems of
steppe grasslands and rich volcanic soils. Brown forest soils have also shown
themselves adaptable to a variety of crops, and are thus attractive to population. On the other hand, the leached soils of temperate lands, the podsols,
can support dense agricultural settlement only after considerable treatment;
in Canada, there is a great contrast between population densities of the Clay
Belt and those of neighbouring podsolic areas. Likewise, most laterites of
the humid tropics are only able to sustain bush fallowing and sparse
populations.

Soil conditions also act as a microfactor affecting in detail the distribution
of particular crops within broad zones, and consequently influencing human
distribution. Grove has described how soils clearly control settlement in
northern Katsina (Nigeria). Brookfield has told a similar story for Mauritius,
and Scott for Tasmania. Examples could be greatly multiplied. We should
also remind ourselves that the attractiveness of soils depends upon man's
agricultural interests and techniques; the light downland soils of Britain
attracted our Neolithic, Bronze Age and Iron Age ancestors, who were
technically incapable of dealing with the forested heavy clay soils of the vales.
In this context and in many others the permeability of soils is significant.

Soil erosion is equally as important as soil fertility in the location of
population. Significant correlations can be made between maps of soil
erosion and population distribution in New Zealand, where nearly one-quarter
of the entire country has been affected by soil erosion. Jacks and Whyte
stress that soil erosion may result either from sparse populations giving

insufficient care to the land, as in the prairies, or from great population pressure on the land, as in the native reserves in the Republic of South Africa. They advocate "the maximum population which the soils can support" as the best insurance against soil erosion.

Biotic Factors

Population distributions respond to the varying distributions of plants and animals, large and small. Selvas, campos, savanna, tundra and taïga offer vastly different media for human occupation and concentration. Forests, grasslands, marshes, deserts and scrub variously assist and deter populations according to their size, spatial relations, vegetational exuberance and character, as well as the techniques and modes of life of indigenous populations. Prairies presented different possibilities to Red Indians and wheat farmers. The forests of Amazonia and Malaya are diversely populated by primitive food gatherers, peasant cultivators and rubber planters. Marshes along the Mediterranean coasts, once malarial wildernesses, are now often closely colonized.

The plant and animal realms are inseparable in their influence upon population; it is the combination of biotic factors which has exerted such pressures: the tsetse flies of the savannas, the locusts of desert fringes, the rabbits of the Australian outback, the mosquitoes of tropical swamps. As civilized man constantly finds new techniques of destroying microbes and parasites, he sets off biological chain reactions, as predators suffer from insufficient prey. Modern man has also found medicines, house designs and other methods of defending himself against parasites. Although he is naturally less adapted to life in humid tropical environments than are their primitive inhabitants, he is better equipped and has more chance of survival than Pygmies or Amazonian Indians.

Disease and Hunger

Mankind has been ravaged and reduced by a wide gamut of diseases, whose distributions vary greatly in time and space, not merely as a result of the diversity of ecological environments but also due to man's mobility and his growing ability to fight against diseases.

Parasitic, bacterial and viral infectious disorders are generally more frequent and severe in the tropics than in temperate zones. High temperatures accelerate biological cycles. Some diseases seem to have natural habitats: trachoma coincides with semi-arid and Mediterranean areas, yellow fever with tropical South America and tropical Africa, sleeping sickness with the domain of the tsetse fly. Some tropical diseases such as malaria have spread into temperate lands and have become endemic there. But the temperate zone is not without its own endemic infections; pest and cholera are obvious examples, now mercifully confined to a few localities in Asia. Tuberculosis, now world-wide, may have originated in the overcrowded conditions of temperate countries and have been spread by Europeans.

While different types of cancer prevail in different parts of the world, there is little evidence to show that the incidence of degenerative diseases is higher in advanced countries than in underdeveloped ones. Similarly, insufficient evidence is available to warrant generalizations about the world distribution of mental ill health.

Nutritional disorders result from a combination of geographical and human conditions. Perhaps two-thirds of mankind suffer from absolute or partial hunger, impairing physique but not reproductive capacity. Specific or partial hungers of protein, minerals or vitamins are caused by dietary deficiencies and may result in severe nutritional diseases. Kwashiorkor is a syndrome specially associated with low protein intake in the tropics. Pellagra results from the shortage of vitamin B_1 in maize-producing areas, and beri-beri from the same shortage in rice-producing areas. Rickets, or "English disease", was common in cold and temperate climates where calcium and vitamin D deficiencies prevailed. Goitre in India and elsewhere results from iodine deficiency. These are some of the obvious signs of malnutrition. Many other infections and infestations result from nutritional inadequacies, curbing the growth and distribution of population, as Josué de Castro so emphatically explained in his *Geography of Hunger*.

The Attraction of Mineral and Energy Resources

Mineral and energy resources exercise a powerful influence upon population distribution wherever there is the requisite technical ability and social organization to exploit the resources. Industrialization naturally increases the significance of minerals in this connexion, but it is far from being an automatic concomitant of mineral extraction.

Minerals vary in their availability, conditions of place-boundness (i.e. availability at one or more sites), mode of extraction, ease of utilization, importance to industrial production, as well as bulk and costs of transportation. So no simple formula can demonstrate their potential power of attraction upon population. In any case, for one reason or another, this potential may never be realized.

Of the energy resources, coal has exerted a much greater stimulus to industrial location than petroleum, natural gas, atomic power or water power. The reasons are varied, but include its great bulk and low value, its utility as a reducer of metals, and its dissipation when used. Nowhere has coal had a greater effect upon population distribution than in Western Europe, although there are obvious signs of its waning significance as hydro-electricity, atomic power, grids, vehicles and petroleum liberate industries and population from coalfield locations.

Non-energy minerals, with the exception of iron ore, have provoked less concentration of industries and population. Again, reasons are varied and manifold: small quantities mined, local concentrations of ores, high value and low transportation costs, or low value and widespread occurrence. Sometimes the location of mines has been unattractive to population. Even iron ore mining has had varying influence; strong in Lorraine, weak in Sierra Leone, for reasons quite apart from the Fe-content of the ores.

The differential attraction of mineral and energy resources upon population cannot be considered without reference to historical developments—indeed, the social, economic and political status of the country or region in which the resources are found.

Population Distribution and Economic Activities

The type and scale of economic activities exercise considerable influence upon population distribution. Among agricultural societies population distribution often responds closely to the nature of staple foods and their relationship to physical conditions. Certain high-yield food crops enable denser populations than others. In contrast, livestock economies are usually associated with sparser populations. Agricultural systems and techniques are also instrumental: wheat farming on the Prairies, rubber planting in Malaya, bush fallowing in West Africa, sheep rearing in New Zealand, rice growing in Asian deltas, and peasant polyculture in Mediterranean Europe are associated with vastly different population distributions. In general, subsistence cultivation shows closer links with land quality than does commercial agriculture, but there are no fixed relationships between types of agriculture and population distribution. Farming varies so much in character and intensity in time and in space. One permissible generalization, however, is that pre-industrial agricultural populations tend to be more evenly distributed than populations with more diverse economic activities. The interconnection of diverse activities stimulates dense population concentrations. The process is generally cumulative until the size of the community presents problems of transportation and overcongestion.

Changes in distribution of population are frequently associated with technological advances. The latter have not only facilitated the settlement of new land areas; through industrialization they have had a contrary influence, in releasing a higher proportion of the population from the land. Localized labour and/or food surpluses were initial stimuli to industrialization, but pre-industrial populations have also influenced industrial location through their consuming power; consumer-orientated industries are sited near dense populations, as in developing countries today.

The Industrial Revolution made sources of energy the great foci of cumulative industrial growth and population concentration. As industrialization proceeds, land and mineral resources have less influence upon general population distribution. Other factors contributing to decreased control of the physical environment are growing spatial mobility of labour, improved transportation, more trade and the diminished importance of place-bound industries. The result is accentuation of the general unevenness of population distributions. But the reduction of rural populations through migration to towns as well as their spread into formerly uncultivated areas has sometimes meant a more even distribution of rural population.

Immobility of labour between industries tends to delay spatial mobility of population, but governments sometimes assist migration of workers. Indeed, government social and economic policies have growing influence upon population distribution. This is particularly true in countries with planned economies where the aim has been more uniformity in levels of regional economic growth, by integrating industrial and agricultural development and providing consumer industries in areas of population concentration. George has stressed that planned socialist redistribution of population leads to a more uniform dispersal.

Commercial activities are closely linked with population concentration and urbanization, and are nowhere more demonstrably significant than in the redistribution of population in developing territories. Here we see in progress the intimate associations between the introduction of a money economy, the establishment of communications, the growth of trading points, migrations of population and urbanization. In Africa today, we find modern equivalents of the old towns of the American West, which were centred on a railway station, hotel, drugstore, a few shops and offices. Local markets, staging posts, and points where there is a change of transport (ports, stations) are the foci of migrations, and here commercial activities are the important criterion of urban status.

Historical and Social Influences

Despite the varied physical and economic influences so far examined, it is obvious that past population distributions influence present and future distributions. In other words, there is a tendency for population distribution inertia. Most distributions are explicable only in terms of the past. The longevity of civilizations in Asia has contributed to present population patterns. Sparse populations in Iraq may be partly attributed to past invasions. Mountain chains in South-West Asia have attracted the pursued and have become populous. Patterns in the Americas owe much to processes of westward colonization, in particular the growth of the railways. In West and East Africa distributions will long retain the effects of slave-raiding and the need for defensive posts. In Europe they still retain the impress of early settlement, enclosures, industrial inertia and the world wars. New Zealand's patterns inevitably reflect something of the origins of the settlers. Likewise, the urban origins of British settlers in Australia must have had some influence on the high urban/rural ratio of that country. In sum, spatial distributions cannot be explained by reference to a given moment in time; they are constantly changing in response to changing human influences and values.

Distributional changes are affected by migrations and by natural movement of population (the interplay of births and deaths). Sometimes migration exceeds natural movement; sometimes the reverse. But all manner of social and political factors affect these two components: cultural difference, religion, social system, class, social services, medical progress, educational level, status of women, national population policies, changes in location and restrictiveness of political boundaries — factors best considered in later chapters.

It should be apparent that interpretation of factors influencing the intricate and mobile patterns of population distribution is no easy task. It involves careful analysis of topographic maps, detailed climatic, economic and social data, a deep knowledge of the past, and an acute awareness of the complexity of forces affecting man's presence on earth. It is all too easy to overemphasize the significance of one factor at the expense of others.

References

BROOKFIELD, H. C., Mauritius: demographic upsurge and prospect, *Pop. Studies*, **2**, 102 (1957).

FOSBERG, F. A. (Ed.), *Man's Place in the Island Ecosystem*, Hawaii, 1965.

GEORGE, P., *Introduction à l'étude géographique de la population du monde*, 1951.

GEORGE, P., *Questions de géographie de la population*, 1959.

GRIGG, D., Degrees of concentration: a note on world population distribution, *Geography*, **54**, 325 (1969).

GROVE, A. T., Soil erosion and population problems in south-east Nigeria, *Geog. J.*, **117**, 291 (1951).

ISARD, W., *Location and Space Economy*, 1956.

JACKS, G. V. and WHYTE, R. O., *Rape of the Earth: A World Survey of Soil Erosion*, 1939.

SCOTT, P., The changing population of Tasmania, *Geog. Studies*, **4**, 13 (1957).

STASZEWSKI, J., Vertical distribution of world population, *Polish Academy of Sciences, Geog. Studies*, **14** (1957).

STASZEWSKI, J., Die Verteilung der Bevölkerung der Erde nach dem Abstand von Meer, *Petermanns Mitteilungen*, **103**, 207 (1959).

STASZEWSKI, J., Bevölkerungsverteilung nach den Klimagebieten von W. Köppen, *Petermanns Mitteilungen*, **105**, 133 (1961).

TREWARTHA, G. T., *A Geography of Population: World Patterns*, 1969.

U.N., *The Determinants and Consequences of Population Trends*, 1953.

CHAPTER IV

MEASURES OF POPULATION DENSITY AND DISTRIBUTION

Areal Distributions

Many attempts have been made to simplify the complexities of population distributions; to extract the bones by statistical analyses. But as compared with most linear distributions, areal distributions are less easy to analyse because of the irregular size of administrative units, the mobility of population and areal variations in the physical environment.

These are also basic problems of population mapping, which attempts a visual presentation of areal data. Subjectivity enters into the preparation of maps through the selection of method (choropleths, isopleths, dots or proportional symbols), class intervals (shading categories, isopleth intervals), and the value, size and location of dots and symbols. Moreover, population maps may not be viewed or evaluated in the way intended by the compiler. However, population mapping cannot concern us here, especially as several excellent texts on cartography deal exhaustively with the subject.

It is important to emphasize that use of the following methods results in both gain and loss. The gain is a different viewpoint of population distribution; the loss is in the inevitable generalization of data. On balance, it is valuable to consider these methods wherever serious analysis of population distribution is necessary.

Population Density

The concept of population density, relating numbers of people to the space occupied by them, is one of the most intriguing and most hazardous correlations employed by geographers. First used in 1837 by Henry Drury Harness in a series of maps for the commission considering the railways of Ireland, it has since developed as a means partly of assessing overpopulation and underpopulation — by comparing existing and potential densities — but mainly of obtaining an index for purposes of areal comparison.

The main difficulties in the use of density indices are:

(a) that population data are available for administrative or census areas rather than for areas of homogeneous economy or population distribution;

28

(b) that such homogeneity is in any case rare;

(c) that densities are merely averages, with all the limitations that this term implies;

(d) that construction of density maps is dependent upon the criteria used in the selection of class intervals;

(e) that interpretation of such maps depends upon the shading method and shading range;

(f) that population numbers can be related to many different measures of space. As Duncan has stated: "any attempt to refine density figures by basing them on 'net' rather than 'gross' area encounters a considerable indeterminacy in the notion of 'net-ness' ".

Despite these criticisms, population density is a useful abstraction, assisting in the analysis of the diversity of man's distribution in space.

We may note that, in general, choropleth maps of population density are preferable to isopleth maps, because density is an areal value rather than a point value, and because they lend themselves more to the depiction of abrupt changes, so characteristic of density (e.g. edge densities of towns).

The man/land ratio is the *crude density of population*, the number of people per unit area. In general, its usefulness is inversely related to the size of the area. Population densities of continents and states conceal too much diversity to be really meaningful. The two most densely populated continents, Europe and Asia, include extremes of density as wide as those in the two most sparsely populated continents, Africa and Australasia. The physical and human conditions of these continents are so disparate and diverse that crude population densities are not comparable. Population densities by national state are comparable where physical conditions are not too dissimilar, but in general crude population densities have more significance for the spatial comparison and differentiation of much smaller units, like parishes or communes, where numbers of people and ranges of environmental and human conditions are much smaller. Certainly they should not be regarded as indices of population pressure, because they do not express functional relationships between population and territory. In this respect they have even less utility for trading economies than for closed economies.

Man/Land Use Densities

As people are congregating more and more into small areas and are leaving so much of the earth's surface sparsely inhabited and little used, it was inevitable that refinements of the density concept should be made, by modifications to the numerator, the denominator or both. The numerator may be either the total population or a category such as rural, agricultural or working population, while the denominator may be the inhabited, rural, cultivable, cultivated or crop areas, or an area weighted according to its land use.

By the dasymetric techniques devised by Wright, densities are calculated only for the inhabited areas, the remaining areas being left blank on population maps. Densities are also calculated for cultivable areas, and are known in France as *physiological densities*. They are preferable to crude densities for a country like Egypt, where 96 per cent of the population inhabit about 4 per cent of the total area, but they must be used judiciously, as land which is not cultivable is not necessarily unproductive. Moreover, in some countries statistics of cultivable land are not available; in others cultivable and cultivated land are not distinguished.

Similar objections may be levelled at indices of population density per unit of cultivated or crop area (which are different in regions of multiple cropping), but they are more realistic indices where agricultural populations are confined to small proportions of total land areas, as in the Caribbean. When only the agricultural population is taken into the calculations, this density is sometimes called the *agricultural density*. In Britain, where less than 5 per cent of the active population are employed in agriculture, the agricultural density may be of greater interest than densities of total population per unit of cultivable or cultivated land. By European standards our agricultural density is very low, and somewhat surprisingly is similar to that of Canada. On the other hand, it is not easy to define the agricultural population. Do we include only active males employed in agriculture, or should we also evaluate the work of women, children and old people, all of whom may play a very useful part in some countries? Whatever the details, comparisons of agricultural densities, say of the Fens and Cheshire Plain, have more interest than comparisons of crude densities.

As cultivable and cultivated areas are not of uniform value, the French geographer Vincent suggested in 1946 an index which he called *comparative density*. It is a type of physiological density, where the total population is related to land area weighted according to its productivity; 1 square kilometre of cultivated land is made equal to 3 square kilometres of grassland. Vincent compiled a world map of comparative density, and considered this density an index of a country's ability to be economically self-sufficient, a condition which had more significance at the time of publication than now. Although in England and Wales we have a very high comparative density, we rely on imports of food from countries like Denmark and The Netherlands, which have lower comparative densities. If agricultural population alone is considered, comparative density has more utility, but not as an index of national autarchy.

This method has been carried a stage further by employing a standard land use unit, termed "a hectare of arable equivalent". All arable land is assumed to be of uniform value; orchards and gardens are three times as valuable as arable land; meadow land has only two-fifths of the value, and pasture only one-fifth. It is doubtful whether calculations of this sort throw more light on the problem of comparison of population densities, as the value of agricultural land varies enormously.

From the point of view of environmental conservation, Allan has proposed a measure of critical density of population (CDP) which he defines as "the human carrying capacity of an area in relation to a given land use system, expressed in terms of population per square mile; it is the maximum population density which a system is capable of supporting permanently in that environment without danger to the land". Three sets of information are used to calculate the CDP: (a) the percentage of land cultivable by traditional methods, (b) the land use factor, or relationship between durations of cultivation and fallow, and (c) cultivation factor, or acreage planted *per capita* each year. It is calculated as $100b \times \frac{c}{a}$. Naturally, these variables are not easy to define accurately, but the CDP is a useful index in the study of subsistence economies.

Economic Density of Population

The notion of economic density of population was proposed in 1934 by the French demographer Simon as a formula

$$\Delta = 100 \, \frac{\delta}{a}$$

where δ is the index of population size and a the general index of production for the same year. Later refinements attempted to relate population to its production capacity, first by incorporating into the formula the index of productivity a',

$$\Delta' = \frac{100\delta}{\left(\dfrac{100a}{a'}\right)},$$

then by replacing the index of production a by an index of latent productivity $a°$:

$$D = \frac{100\delta}{\dfrac{100a°}{a'}}$$

$$\therefore \frac{D}{\Delta'} = \frac{a}{a°}$$

$$\Delta' = \frac{a°}{a}D.$$

Simon believed that he had discovered an index capable of determining the optimum density population in relation to a base period. If Δ' exceeded D and $a°$ exceeded a there was a tendency to under-production and under-population; if they were equal there was an optimum population.

As other denominators in his formula, instead of the general index of production, Simon also proposed (a) the general index of consumption, and (b) the general index of all economic activities. Further denominators suggested are (c) average income per person, (d) standard of living, and (e) available diets. George has insisted that such measures of economic wealth are inadequate unless examined in the light of the different economic systems and of social evolution. He states that the index of national income masks the real standards of living of the various social classes. Furthermore, the calculation of these denominators is vitiated by changing international conditions.

Although these complicated formulae have some utility for comparisons in time within one country, they cannot easily be used for international comparisons. Thus the concept of density has been extended beyond the scope of geography. Indeed, the density concept has passed from the notion of intensity of occupation of space to one of density of standards of living. Cause and effect relationships are consequently confused.

Persons per Room

The usual concept of population density as the ratio between population and land area has less significance for industrial and urban populations than for those which are largely agricultural and rural. In the calculation of urban population densities a variety of denominators may be used, such as (a) total urban area, (b) built-up area, (c) net area of occupied dwelling lots and incidental service uses, and (d) gross area of occupied dwelling lots and incidental service uses (including streets, parks, etc.). However, these densities throw little light on congestion within towns, where vertical expansion partially invalidates man/land ratios, and tell us nothing about the concentration of people within buildings; within houses and rooms. In countries where people spend a considerable part of their lives indoors, this concentration has great interest to the population geographer.

In Britain, Ireland and some other countries data are available of the average numbers of persons per room for all administrative units. These averages, sometimes termed room densities, are useful indices of density of occupation as well as housing conditions. Unfortunately, they ignore the sizes of rooms, an important factor when one considers that rooms are often smallest where room densities are highest, as in tenements. Persons per room data are normally limited to private households, the size and composition of which are not taken into account by room densities.

Census reports also provide data of the number and percentage of private households (and/or of the population of private households) living at different room densities. Only habitable rooms are counted, namely usual living rooms, including bedrooms and kitchens, but excluding sculleries, bathrooms, etc., and any warehouse, office, shop rooms.

Persons per room indices reflect intercensal changes in housing conditions as well as regional and rural/urban variations in these conditions. Until the 1961 census in Britain, the average density of two persons per room was considered the lower level of overcrowding, but the rapid and persistent decline in room densities and overcrowding led to the use of $1\frac{1}{2}$ persons per room as a more valid index in England, Wales and Scotland.

Figure 3 demonstrates some of the regional differences in persons per room and overcrowding in Britain at the 1951 census. Scottish figures were much higher than those of England — Irish room densities were even higher — and central Scotland was the main "black spot". Very low room densities (less than 0·7 person per room) were found in central and west Wales, south-west England and large parts of south-eastern England. In Scotland, the Clydeside conurbation and the main cities had much higher densities than the small burghs andl andward (= rural) population, but in England and Wales there was little tendency for room density to increase with the size of the urban area. The maps of rooms per house and persons per household, especially the former, indicate the two major influences upon room densities and overcrowding, but other influences may be invoked: the proportions in the various social classes, occupational and industrial compositions, age and sex structures, size and composition of families, and traditions of house construction.

Central Tendency of Population Distributions

A number of centrographical methods are used to describe the central tendency, centrality or average position of populations. They were developed mostly in the 1920s and early 1930s by the Russian geographer Sviatlovsky, who was concerned with determining the central point of population in the U.S.S.R.

The *mean centre* or *mean point* of population has also been variously called the centroid, centre of gravity or balancing point. It is the fulcrum of a distribution where each unit is considered to have equal weight on a hypothetical rigid level plane, and, as Hart describes in detail, may be located by determining the point of intersection of two lines along which the plane would balance. In different terms, it is the point about which distances measured to all the individuals of the population will, when squared, add up to a minimum value. The mean centre is the equivalent for an areal distribution of the arithmetic mean for a linear distribution. It may be

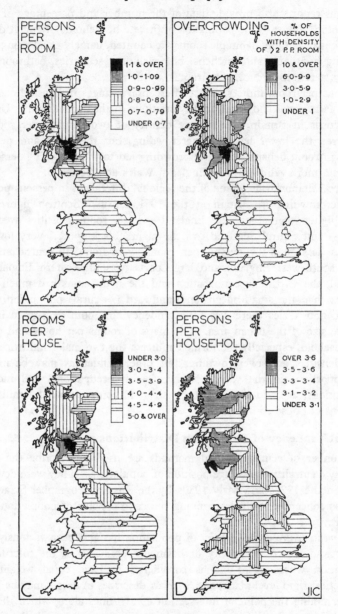

FIG. 3. Room density, number of rooms and size of household in Great Britain, 1951. Data are by counties, and there have since been considerable changes.

described for grouped data as $\Sigma(pr^2)$ where Σ means the sum of, p equals the population within a segment of area, and r is the distance of the mid-point of the segment to the point in question.

Of the various measures of central tendency, the mean centre is the most useful for studying areal shifts in distribution over a period of time. Like the arithmetic mean of linear distributions, its main disadvantage is that it is greatly affected by extreme or remote values. Perth, for example, exerts a disproportionate influence upon the mean centre of population in Australia, as does Vancouver in Canada.

The *median centre* of population, or centre of convergence, is the point where the whole population could be assembled with the minimum aggregate travel distance. For grouped data $\Sigma(pr)$ is appropriate. It was long thought that the median centre could only be found by calculating the aggregate travel distance for several points and then by finding the centre by trial and error; Hart suggested the use of a transparent mask of concentric circles (annule mask) to assist in its location. Porter has shown recently that the convergence point can be accurately determined by means of "least-squares" analysis. In his theory of median location, Quinn considered the median centre an optimum location for centralized services, although factors like site, ancillary facilities and market potential may be equally important. Some have called it "fun with geometry", but as Porter has suggested, it may be used to advantage with time-series maps for summarizing locational changes.

The *median point* differs from the median centre, in being the intersection of two orthogonal lines each dividing the population into two equal groups. If the lines are rotated the location of the point changes. Lines may be drawn parallel to them to divide the population into quarters in each direction, the points of intersection being termed *quartilides*. Further indications of dispersion may be realized by the calculation of *decilides* and *centilides*. The median point is equally influenced by every individual in the distribution, and so is less influenced by extremes than is the mean centre. The median point also remains unaffected by movements within the distribution and is more stable than the mean centre. It is thus the best index of centrality for a distribution, and is most useful for comparing different distributions in the same area at the same time. Hart also suggests that it is probably preferable to the mean centre as a control point for plotting isopleths in areas of uneven distributions.

The *modal centre* of population refers to the maximum surface density. Its position may be affected by the sizes of areas considered. In all large populations it coincides with the principal peak of the population potential, discussed later in this chapter. Most countries are uni-modal: London, Paris and Buenos Aires are striking examples of uni-modal centres in their respective countries, though at a lower level many of the new capitals of

Africa exhibit this tendency. Occasionally, we find bi-modal centres: Sao Paulo and Rio de Janeiro in Brazil, Sydney and Melbourne in Australia, and Montreal and Toronto in Canada. Multi-modal distributions are less common, though there are tendencies in this direction in India, New Zealand and The Netherlands. In general, the concept of the mode is less valuable in areal distributions than in linear distributions.

These are not the only possible centrographical measures. We may determine an harmonic mean centre and a geometric mean centre, but these are less easily understood. The former is located where the reciprocal of the sum of the reciprocals of the distances to units of the population is at a minimum.

The diverse mathematical properties of the above measures result in different utilities and locations. In the United States the mean centre has constantly moved westward along the 39th parallel pursued by the median centre and median point, while the mode and harmonic mean centre remain in New York. It may seem that these centrographic measures are of only academic interest, but they may be of practical utility, especially in the development plans of emergent nations. In circular Sierra Leone, for example, it is useful to study centrality in order to decide where to locate new schools, hospitals and other social amenities.

Measures of Dispersion of Population

Various statistical methods may be employed in the study of population dispersion, which is complementary to the study of central tendency. Warntz and Neft have shown that the various measures of dispersion are analogous to a series of statistical *moments*, which can be computed about any point.

The *standard distance deviation*, proposed as an ecological index by Lefever in 1926, has been developed by Stewart and Warntz as the *dynamical radius* of a population, measuring, for example, the expansion of the population of the United States (see Fig. 4). Similar to the standard deviation of linear distributions, the standard distance deviation is found by dividing the mean centre $\Sigma(pr^2)$ — defined earlier in this chapter — by the total population (P) and then by taking the square root of the resulting mean square

$$S_r = \sqrt{\frac{\Sigma(pr^2)}{P}}.$$

The *second moment* is employed in the derivation of the standard distance deviation. Isolines of *aggregate squared-distance deviations* are concentric circles about the mean centre, regardless of population distribution.

The *mean distance deviation* is likewise the counterpart of the mean deviation of linear statistics, and it measures the arithmetic mean distance of individuals

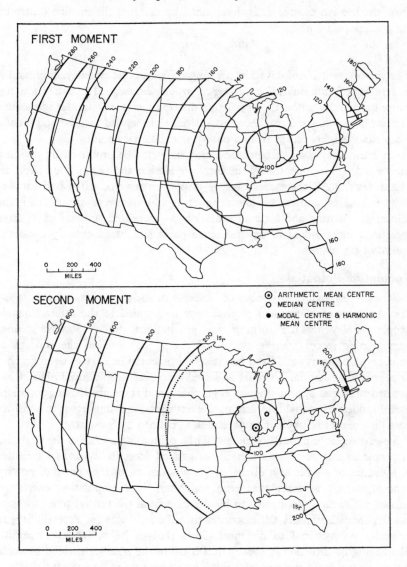

FIG. 4. The first and second moments of population in the United States, 1950. The first moment or aggregate travel distance is in units of one thousand million persons times miles. The value at any point represents the arithmetic mean distance in miles required to move everyone in the population to that point by the shortest route. The second moment is in units of one thousand million persons times miles-squared about the mean centre. Also shown is the standard distance deviation. After WARNTZ, W. and NEFT, D., Contributions to a statistical methodology for areal distributions, *J. Regional Science*, **2**, 63 (1960).

from the median centre. It is determined by dividing the median centre by
the total population:

$$\text{md}_r = \frac{\Sigma(pr)}{P}$$

The *first moment* is employed in deriving the mean distance deviation, and it
is represented by isolines of *aggregate travel distance*. The latter are not
concentric circles unless the population distribution exerts circular symmetry.
It must be emphasized that the practical value of maps of the first and second
moments is slight, except from a purely statistical viewpoint.

An harmonic mean distance deviation may also be produced by dividing
the harmonic mean centre by the total population and taking the reciprocal
of the result. All three measures of dispersion may be calculated for any
point in an area, and each is lowest about its appropriate centre, which is the
minimum. Warntz and Neft have described generalized versions of all three
measures, independent of any reference point and based entirely upon the
spread of population.

Population Potential

Stewart formulated a number of concepts in social physics, which suggest
that the laws of Newtonian physics may be applied to the interactions of
people. Following the formula for gravitational force, Stewart defines
demographic force; from gravitational energy he develops the concept of
demographic energy; and from gravitational potential he derives demographic
or population potential. It must be stated that macroscopic social physics has
not had universal appeal among geographers, and some are looking for more
useful models of spatial interaction. Nevertheless, it is important to consider
here the concept of population potential, as defined by Stewart.

Stewart refers to population potential of a point as a measure of the nearness
of people to that point, as a measure of general accessibility or as a measure
of influence of people at a distance. He was critical of the centre of gravity
concept, which assumes that each individual in a population exerts an
influence directly proportional to his distance from the central point. Population potential assumes the opposite, that the influence (or accessibility) is
inversely proportional to distance. It is said to be a "scalar" quantity
(i.e. having no direction in space), and equal to the number divided by their
distance away from the central point. At a given point, the potential is the
sum of the reciprocals of the distances of all individuals from the point.
With grouped data, population potential at a point may be described as
$\Sigma(p/r)$, using the same symbols as earlier in this chapter. Isopleths of potential
(equipotential lines) are interpolated on a map after initial plotting of
significant points. Unlike the concept of population density, population
potential has point significance.

The notion of population potential bears a close relationship to aggregate travel distance as well as to the harmonic mean centre, which coincides with the peak of population potential. Indeed, the harmonic mean distance of the population from a point is the reciprocal of the potential there divided by the total population. A further correlation, which in this case has no mathematical basis, is that between population density and population potential; this correlation is marked in the United States and in England and Wales, as seen in Fig. 5.

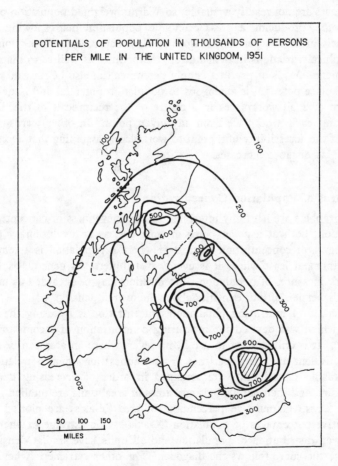

POTENTIALS OF POPULATION IN THOUSANDS OF PERSONS PER MILE IN THE UNITED KINGDOM, 1951

Fig. 5. Equipotential lines in thousands of persons per mile in the United Kingdom, 1951. Population potential ranges from less than 100,000 per mile in the Shetlands to more than 1,900,000 in the London Basin. After STEWART, J. Q. and WARNTZ, W., Physics of population distribution, *J. Regional Science*, **1,** 110 (1958).

The concept of population potential is more useful than that of aggregate travel distance, and has sometimes proved valuable as an indicator of geographical variations in social and economic phenomena, e.g. rural population density, farmland values, miles of railway track per square mile, road density, density of wage earners in manufacturing, and death rates. Rural density, for example, tends to be proportional to the square of the potential.

As all people do not have the same statistical "weight", Stewart proposed that this weight should be represented by the "social mass per capita" — whatever is artificially produced or transported for social purposes. Data of social mass are not readily available, so Warntz weighted population potential by income, producing a gross economic population map showing income potentials in dollars per mile (Fig. 6). This map revealed a relationship to geographical variations in demand for commodities as well as to many other phenomena. Maps of product supply potentials can also be drawn.

Workplace potential is analogous to population potential and is defined as the sum over all workplaces in a centre of the reciprocals of the distances separating each workplace from any given point. In other words, it is an index of the accessibility of a point to workplaces, assuming that accessibility declines as distance increases.

Measures of Population Concentration

Geographers are naturally interested in the unevenness or concentration of population, both at a given point in time and as an evolutionary process. The degree of concentration is greatest where a population is assembled at one point, and least where it is evenly distributed. In general, as Duncan has said, measures of population concentration may be regarded as measures of the dispersion of unit densities about the overall density.

A method of measuring population concentration is by using the Lorenz curve, which was devised for measuring concentration of income or wealth (Fig. 7). It is only correct to use it, however, where an area can be divided into equivalent units (e.g. parishes or communes) for which population data are available. Areal units are arranged in order of decreasing density of population, and then populations and areas of areal units are totalled for each density class. Cumulative percentages of area (Y-axis) are plotted against cumulative percentages of population (X-axis). One extreme is where there is an even distribution of population and all units have similar densities; in this case the curve follows the diagonal. The other extreme is where population is concentrated at one point; then the curve coincides with the X-axis. Between these extremes, degrees of uneven spread of population are depicted by the departure of the curve from the diagonal. The slope of the tangent of the curve of concentration at a point gives a measure of the density at that point, and where this slope is 45° (the slope of the diagonal of equal distribution) the density is the general average of the area considered. Concentration

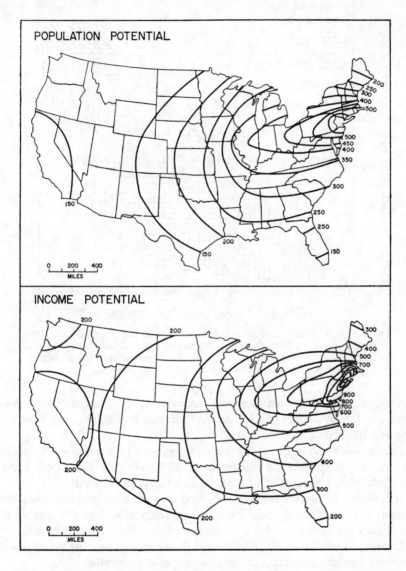

FIG. 6. Population potential and income potential of the United States, 1950. Population potential is in units of one thousand persons per mile. Income potential is in millions of dollars per mile, although local city peaks are not shown. After WARNTZ, W. and NEFT, D., *op. cit.* and STEWART, J. Q. and WARNTZ, W., Macrogeography and Social Science, *Geog. Review,* **48,** 167 (1958).

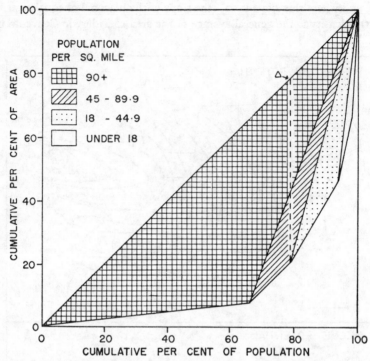

FIG. 7. Lorenz curve of population concentration in the United States, 1950, in relation to density intervals on a county basis. The index of concentration Δ is also marked. After DUNCAN, O. D., The measurement of population distribution, *Population Studies*, **11**, 29 (1957–8).

curves of succeeding censuses are comparable; but, as De Smet has noted, if the populations of all areal units increase at the same rate, then the concentration curve will not change.

Gini's *concentration ratio* (CR) was also suggested for measuring inequality of income. It expresses the area on the graph between the Lorenz curve and the diagonal as a proportion of the total area below the diagonal.

The *index of concentration* is the maximum vertical distance from the Lorenz curve to the diagonal. Its value is directly related to the number of areal units and inversely related to the size of the units. All indices must be considered in relation to the number and dimensions of areal units; no index provides a unique indication of the character of concentration.

Wright examined in detail coefficients of unevenness of distributions, which depend upon the form of the Lorenz curve and upon its deviation from the diagonal. In particular, he took the area between the Lorenz curve and the horizontal and vertical axes, an area which is an isosceles triangle when the population is evenly distributed. The variable dimensions of triangles may be related to the maximum area of uniform distribution, and the coefficient R varies from 0 to 1, from minimum to maximum evenness. Wright also sought to define a factor of relative concentration, C, to enable distinction between Lorenz curves with the same coefficient of evenness (i.e. delimiting similar areas).

De Smet found that although the coefficients R and C provide valuable indications of the distribution of densities in relation to the average density, they are independent of the geographic distribution of densities. The same values of R and C apply to an infinite number of geographic distributions. Using a method derived from the Wentworth method of average slope determination, De Smet superimposed a square mesh on a density map, added up the differences in density changes along each line of squares in two directions, and divided the total by the length of the lines. The resulting coefficient, P, supplements those of Wright.

Measures of Population Spacing

A measure of the spacing of population units was devised by Clark and Evans for ecological distributions, and is known as the *mean distance between nearest neighbours*. This concept is based on the assumption of random distribution, and the methods are only appropriate where random variables have generated a distribution. A further disadvantage of this approach in studies of the distribution of human populations is that computations cannot be made from grouped data. Duncan considered the method "more useful for tendencies toward uniformity than for discriminating among patterns of aggregation". Studies by Dacey and King in the United States have supported the view that the settlement pattern approximates to a random distribution, although Dacey has shown that smaller settlements reveal signs of a more regular pattern than do larger settlements.

Barnes and Robinson devised a linear distance map for revealing variations in density of relatively dispersed populations. Average distance between farmhouses equals $1 \cdot 11 / \sqrt{\text{density}}$, density being taken as the number of farmhouses per square mile. Mather has corrected the constant to $1 \cdot 07$. The linear distance map relates the concepts of spacing and density.

Measures of Spatial Association

Geographical patterns of aspects of population composition (see Chapter VI) can be analysed by a number of statistical indices. Several are derived from the *index of dissimilarity*, which gives a description of the association between two distributions over a group of areal units. It is one-half the sum of the absolute differences between two populations, taken area by area, and therefore shows the percentage of the one population who would have to move into other areas in order to have a similar percentage distribution of population.

When the index of dissimilarity is calculated between a sub-group of the population and the rest of the population, this is known as an *index of segregation*, as it shows the degree of segregation of the sub-group. Other indices of segregation have been devised, and are examined in a paper by Duncan and Duncan.

Slightly different in purpose is the *location quotient*, which describes the relative concentration of two populations within a single area. It is merely the ratio between the percentage of one population living within a given area and the percentage of another population within that area. When the quotient is one, the two populations are equally represented.

References

ALLAN, W., *The African Husbandman*, 1965.

BARNES, J. A. and ROBINSON, A. H., A new method for the representation of dispersed rural settlement, *Geog. Review*, **30**, 134 (1940).

CLARK, P. J. and EVANS, F. C., Distance to nearest neighbour as a measure of spatial relationships in populations, *Ecology*, **35**, 445 (1954).

CLARKE, J. I., Persons per room: an index of population density, *Tijdschrift voor Economische en Sociale Geografie*, **51**, 257 (1960).

DACEY, M. F., *Analysis of Central Place and Point Patterns by a Nearest Neighbour Model*, Lund Studies in Geography, Series B, **24**, 55 (1962).

DE SMET, R. E., Degré de concentration de la population, *Revue Belge de Géographie*, **86**, 39 (1962).

DUNCAN, O. D., The measurement of population distribution, *Population Studies*, **11**, 27 (1957–8).

DUNCAN, O. D. and DUNCAN, B., A methodological analysis of segregation indices, *Amer. Sociological Review*, **20**, 210 (1955).

GEORGE, P., Sur un projet de calcul d'une densité économique, *Bull. de l'Assoc. des Géographes Français*, **237-8**, 142.

HART, J. F., Central tendency in areal distributions, *Econ. Geog.*, **30**, 48 (1954).

KING, L. J., A quantitative expression of the pattern of urban settlements in selected areas of the United States, *Tijdschrift voor Economische en Sociale Geografie*, **53**, 1 (1962).

LAWTON, R., A map of overcrowding in the British Isles, *Trans. and Papers Inst. Brit. Geographers*, **43** (1968).

PORTER, P. W., What is the point of minimum aggregate travel? *Ann. Assoc. Amer. Geographers*, **53**, 224 (1963).

QUINN, J. A., The hypothesis of median location, *Amer. Sociological Review*, **8**, 148 (1943).

ROBINSON, A. H. *et al.*, A correlation and regression analysis applied to rural farm population densities in the Great Plains, *Ann. Assoc. Amer. Geographers*, **51**, 211 (1961).

SIMON, P., Indices de densité économique de population: méthodes de calcul et applications, *Population*, **1**, 49 (1945).

STEWART, J. Q., Empirical mathematical rules concerning the distribution and equilibrium of population, *Geog. Review*, **37**, 461 (1947).

STEWART, J. Q. and WARNTZ, W., Macrogeography and Social Science, *Geog. Review*, **48**, 167 (1958).

STEWART, J. Q. and WARNTZ, W., Physics of population distribution, *J. Regional Science*, **1**, 99 (1958).

STEWART, J. Q. and WARNTZ, W., Some parameters of the geographical distribution of population, *Geog. Review*, **49**, 270 (1959).

SVIATLOVSKY, E. E. and EELS, W. C., The centrographical method and regional analysis, *Geog. Review*, **27**, 240 (1937).

WARNTZ, W., A new map of the surface of population potentials for the United States, 1960, *Geog. Review*, **54**, 170 (1964).

WARNTZ, W. and NEFT, D., Contributions to a statistical methodology for areal distributions, *J. Regional Science*, **2**, 47 (1960).

WRIGHT, J. K., Some measures of distributions, *Ann. Assoc. Amer. Geographers*, **27**, 177 (1937).

CHAPTER V

URBAN AND RURAL POPULATIONS

URBAN populations differ strongly from rural populations in distribution, density, ways of life, structure and growth. Some of these differences will be examined in later chapters. Here we must focus on the definitions of urban and rural, the process of urbanization, and the size and distribution of urban and rural populations. However, we must avoid excessive encroachment into the realms of urban geography, which in Western countries is considered external to population geography.

Urban–Rural Classification

Distinction between urban and rural is a thorny problem for the population geographer. Sociologists consider urban population in terms of town living, that is to say the concentration of dwellings in a recognizable street pattern, where people live in some social and economic interdependence, enjoying common administrative, cultural and social amenities. We read that "urbanism, the culture of cities, is a way of life". But such a definition is too vague for statistical analysis. Others may prefer to base their definition on the type of land use or the activities of the population.

There are certain inherent difficulties in urban–rural classification of population. First, it is no easy task to draw a line between what is urban and what is rural. There exists a wide range of settlement patterns between the two, especially in advanced countries. There towns are increasingly tentacular and large communities exist in the urban–rural fringe, where urban and rural cultures merge. Among such communities are many people who live in apparently rural areas, but are fully integrated into the urban economic system, and the problem of identifying such people has encouraged the analysis of the city-region as a meaningful index of urban population. Moreover, it is not surprising that in the United States it is customary to break down the urban population into "metropolitan" and "other urban", and the rural population into "rural-farm" and "rural-nonfarm". The rural-nonfarm category, introduced in 1920 and growing steadily, includes non-agricultural workers, such as miners, foresters, fishermen, and workers in hotels, garages, shops and offices, all of whom now exceed the rural-farm population.

Secondly, towns vary enormously in character and function; there are, for example, few features common to Arab *medinas*, French seaside resorts, British textile towns, African mining towns, Australian state capitals, and Indian hill stations. Thirdly, population data are normally available only for administrative units, whose boundaries may not coincide at all with the limits between town and country. Furthermore, the size of such units varies greatly from state to state. Fourthly, there are wide national variations in urban–rural classification, which inhibit international comparisons.

Four general approaches are usually employed by the various censuses for classifying the population as urban or rural. The first is the classification of administrative divisions in which the populations of the divisions are classified as urban or rural on the basis of selected criteria:

(a) type of local government (e.g. Australia, Canada, Ceylon, New Zealand, Republic of South Africa, United Kingdom);

(b) total number of inhabitants of the minor administrative divisions (e.g. Austria, Belgium, Czechoslovakia, Germany, Netherlands, Spain, Switzerland);

(c) the size of the principal cluster of the minor administrative divisions (e.g. France, Luxembourg, Greece).

Administrative or legal definitions only prove satisfactory where there is constant review of boundaries and locality sizes, and the example of the United Kingdom demonstrates that the local government map is not very effective in distinguishing between urban and rural.

The second method classifies administrative centres of all minor divisions as urban and the remainders as rural. Countries which have used this type of classification include Brazil, Colombia, Honduras, Peru, Guatemala, Egypt and Turkey. Peru and Turkey have also added to the urban category places with more than a certain number of inhabitants.

The third method is the classification of agglomerations or population clusters, where the urban population is identified as the residents of closely settled localities, places or centres above a given size. The minimum size varies greatly: Denmark 200, Albania 400, Chile 1000, Argentina and Portugal 2000, Mexico and Venezuela 2500, Iran 5000. In this method the official boundaries of administrative divisions are not usually considered, so the main problem is the identification and delimitation of agglomerations or population clusters in the census. Different methods may be used. Population density is a possible criterion, but in a sense this is putting the cart before the horse as density cannot be computed until limits have been set. The presence of certain institutionalized services (telephones, public utilities, schools, market places, etc.) may also be used as a criterion. But there can be no rules about the identification of population clusters.

The fourth method is based on the assumption that a town may be more suitably differentiated from rural centres by the presence of non-agricultural activities, and the official definitions of urban status in countries like Israel, Jordan and Yugoslavia include such a criterion. In advanced countries such activities frequently occur in villages, but a certain concentration of them is necessary for urban status. The presence of industry may be another criterion, but some towns have no industries and some industries are unaccompanied by urban development. In underdeveloped countries many substantial pre-industrial towns are largely inhabited by people living from agriculture. Such centres may have far fewer urban functions and amenities than quite small trading centres established at crossroads.

It is evident that the above methods of approach mean wide variations in minimum urban sizes ranging from 200 in Finland and Sweden to 30,000 in Japan. Some countries use combinations of methods; the United States now defines urban areas as incorporated places of 2500 or more inhabitants and the urban fringes of cities of 50,000 or more. On the other hand, some underdeveloped countries have no formal definition of urban status at all. In the face of a bewildering array of classifications, the United Nations have suggested that no attempt be made to distinguish between urban and rural, and have recommended that population should be classed according to the following sizes: (1) 500,000 inhabitants and over; (2) 100,000 to 500,000; (3) 25,000 to 100,000; (4) 10,000 to 25,000; (5) 5000 to 10,000; (6) 2000 to 5000; (7) 1000 to 2000; (8) 500 to 1000; (9) less than 500; (10) population not in identifiable agglomerations or clusters. Indeed there is a growing body of opinion that, in developed countries at least, the urban and rural worlds are not dichotomous, but a continuum. It has been shown, for example, in the United States that rural populations in areas under the immediate influence of urban centres differ considerably from populations in more remote rural areas, being much more unstable and dynamic. This interdependence of town and country has led many authors to doubt the utility of urban–rural classification.

Built-up Areas

The urban area rarely coincides with the built-up area or urbanized territory. There are cases (e.g. Cordoba and Zaragoza in Spain) where the former is over one hundred times larger than the latter, and others where suburbs are omitted entirely.

In Britain a special study was carried out for the census of 1951, which distinguished as "urbanized land" any (urban) ward or (rural) civil parish, of which any part was "built up". Definition of the latter was 10 people or more to the acre. In 1951, more than $\frac{1}{2}$ million of the $31\frac{1}{2}$ million urbanized population lived in rural administrative areas, and nearly $4\frac{1}{2}$ million of the

12 million non-urbanized population lived in urban administrative areas. In other words, more people lived in non-urbanized land in urban administrative areas than in urbanized land in rural administrative areas, so the urban–rural ratio based on local authorities is exaggerated.

Urban–Rural Ratios

Analysis of the problems of urban–rural classification indicates that the ratio of urban to rural population may be of little value for international comparisons, even where the same criteria are used. Authors seeking inter-national comparisons have generally used a standard size category, such as the population living in places with more than 20,000 or 100,000 inhabitants — a technique with obvious limitations. Urban–rural ratios obviously have greater accuracy within a state, where criteria and conditions of urbanization are more uniform. In such cases simple statistical mapping (e.g. divided circles) can demonstrate regional variations in ratios.

Nevertheless, it is apparent that there is a wide gap between countries like Britain and Israel which are four-fifths urban, and African agricultural countries, like Kenya, Uganda, Tanzania and Sudan where urban popu-lations amount to less than one-tenth of the total population. Other West European countries with high urban–rural ratios are The Netherlands, Belgium, West Germany, France, Finland, Sweden, Austria and Denmark. Australia, New Zealand and the United States are also highly urbanized, partly as a consequence of the transplantation of urbanism from Europe; in all three, urbanization contrasts strongly with sparse rural populations. Newcomers to the list of countries which are over 50 per cent urban are Japan, Mexico, Argentina, Venezuela, Chile and Uruguay.

Urbanization

Unfortunately the term "urbanization", like many others, suffers from a confusing variety of definitions, including the following six which have been commonly used by geographers:
   (a) the proportion of the total population in an area living in urban centres;
   (b) the number of people in an area living in urban centres;
   (c) the growth in the proportion of the total population in an area living in urban centres;
   (d) the growth in the number of people in an area living in urban centres;
   (e) the social process by which urbanism is introduced to a population;
   (f) the physical spread of urban land.
The situation has also been further complicated by the fact that many authors using the term have provided no definition at all.

It has also been argued that there is very little relationship between physical urbanization and population growth—that in many urban centres there has been urban expansion without any associated population expansion while in other urban centres there has been population expansion without any associated urban expansion. Therefore population growth is not necessarily a good index of urban growth, if the latter is viewed as the urbanization of the land rather than of the people.

One rather obvious point, but worthy of note as it is often ignored, is that trends in the urbanization of people follow a logistic curve, in which the rate of increase in urbanization diminishes as the proportion rises.

This is not the place to discuss in detail the processes of urbanization, especially in an historical context. We may note, however, that in pre-industrial civilizations the scale and proportion of urbanization were much less important than among industrial societies. Indeed, large-scale urbanization is mainly a product of social and economic forces operating in the nineteenth and twentieth centuries: industrialization, its commercial ramifications and the expansion of European civilization. The upsurge of cities in such widely separated countries as Australia, Argentina and Japan results from the same forces, and, moreover, the demographic processes are often similar. Too often urbanization seems to be the snowballing of the large cities at the expense not only of rural areas, but also of small towns.

Gibbs has suggested that population concentration follows an order of five stages:

STAGE I: Towns emerge, but the increase rate of the rural population equals or exceeds the increase rate of the urban population. The urban–rural ratio is greatly influenced by food supply and by transportation technology.

STAGE II: The rate of increase of the urban population exceeds that of the rural population, largely because of rural–urban migration, although the impetus is provided by improvements in food supply and transportation. This stage also reflects the accumulations of the slow urban growth of Stage I, and thus fairly large cities appear, with a high degree of division of labour.

STAGE III: Rural–urban migration exceeds the diminishing natural increase of the rural population, which experiences an absolute decline.

STAGE IV: As the volume of rural–urban migration dwindles, the large centres exert a powerful attraction upon small towns, which become the new source of migrants. Their population ultimately declines.

STAGE V: Concentration does not persist until all are congregated in one huge urban centre. Improvements in communications enable populations to exist without a high degree of concentration and so there is an outward movement or residential dispersion from areas of high density. Areal distribution of population is thus more even, because of the increased population of areas distant from the major population centres. New urban centres may arise. This deconcentration should not be confused with decentralization within urban areas, which may occur while concentration is in progress.

Gibbs states that the order will only appear without exception in closed populations, that it is neither inevitable nor irreversible, and that the stages are not mutually exclusive. A society may be in Stages III and IV at the same time, but it is unlikely that it will enter Stage IV before Stage III.

Some may regard the theory as lacking in practical utility, because no population is completely indigenous and isolated, and none follows entirely the sequence hypothesized. On the other hand, the theory finds some validity in large national units.

Consideration of the relationship between urbanization and industrialization has led some authors to suggest that the level of urbanization in some countries, like Egypt and South Korea, is higher than one would expect, and they have been described as over-urbanized. The explanation given for this phenomenon is that the "push" of migrants from densely peopled, poor rural areas has been strong. Sovani has demonstrated that the relationship between urbanization and industrialization has been closer in underdeveloped countries than in advanced countries, but it has been argued that this may be just one stage in the urban history of these countries and that in any case urbanization in underdeveloped countries may in future be much more closely related to commercial and administrative functions. A lack of correlation between urbanization and industrialization may not be therefore necessarily unhealthy.

Frequency Distribution of Towns by Size

The urban–rural ratio of a country may have little relation to the frequency distribution of towns by size. Owing to varied definitions of urban status, international comparisons are sometimes hazardous, though such comparisons are desirable. Size classes may be expressed cumulatively for purposes of comparison, as in Table 5.1.

TABLE 5.1. DISTRIBUTION OF AGGLOMERATIONS IN AUSTRALIA (1947) AND INDIA (1951)

Size classes	% of agglom. pop. in each class and over		% of aggloms. in each class and over	
	Australia	India	Australia	India
2,000 – 4,999	100·0	100·0	100·0	100·0
5,000 – 9,999	89·5	56·0	33·1	18·1
10,000 – 19,999	83·1	40·6	14·4	5·7
20,000 – 49,999	77·3	31·9	6·3	2·3
50,000 – 99,999	70·7	23·1	2·4	0·7
100,000+	69·3	17·5	2·1	0·3

Population Geography

Often more profitable is the comparison of absolute frequency distributions of successive censuses, as in Table 5.2.

TABLE 5.2. POPULATION IN LOCALITIES BY SIZE CLASS, CANADA, 1956 AND 1661

Size of locality	Census, 1956		Census, 1961	
	Number	Population	Number	Population
500,000 or more	2	1,777,145	2	1,863,469
100,000 – 499,999	9	1,884,849	10	2,290,872
50,000 – 99,999	12	769,323	17	1,134,214
10,000 – 49,999	114	2,310,767	145	3,037,484
5,000 – 9,999	117	830,289	132	932,936
1,000 – 4,999	580	1,269,831	616	1,372,666
Below 1,000	1039	443,922	1039	437,207

In order to take account of the urban size hierarchy in the analysis of urbanization, rather than rely on the proportion or number of people in localities above a certain size threshold, Gibbs has proposed a *scale of urbanization*. The formula is $Su = \Sigma XY$ where Su is the measure, X is the proportion of the urban population in units above a certain size and Y is the proportion of the total population in the same units. The scale of urbanization therefore considers the frequency distribution of both the urban and the total population. The minimum value approaches 0.000 while the maximum is 1.000 (N) where N is the number of size classes. An expression of the actual value as a percentage of the maximum yields a relative measure of the scale of urbanization. In calculations Gibbs advises standardization of size classes, and the largest class must not be too large.

Gibbs has also proposed another measure of urbanization reflecting the urban size hierarchy, the *scale of population concentration*, which is the sum of the proportion of the total population in each class and over. Again it can be expressed as a percentage of the possible, giving a relative measure of the scale of population concentration.

Empirical observation tends to suggest that there is a high degree of association between the degree of urbanization (or urban–rural ratio), the scale of urbanization and the scale of population concentration, possibly because larger urban units tend to be increasing more rapidly than smaller units. On the other hand, Berry has observed through statistical analysis that there is no relationship between town-size distribution and the degree of urbanization, because the former is a product of history and functioning of an urban system rather than the amount of urban development.

Measures of central tendency of town sizes include the mean size, which is often fairly close to the lower limit of town size, and the median size, which is found by arraying locality data in order of size and by taking the middle value. The *equatorial community size* divides arrayed population data in half. In 1961 one-half of the population of England and Wales lived in urban areas of 67,000 inhabitants or more.

The Rank–Size Rule and Urban Hierarchy

The frequencies of town sizes in different territories are fairly closely comparable. In general, the number of small towns exceeds the number of medium-size towns, which outnumber the large towns. When towns are arranged in order of size, it is postulated that there is an empirical relationship between the rank of a town and its population size. When frequency distributions are plotted on double logarithmic graph paper they are linear and concave upward (Fig. 8). This empirical relationship is termed the rank–size rule, first presented by Auerbach in a study of German cities. Lotka later found that the law of urban concentration indicated by the hundred largest cities of the United States was:

$$(\text{rank})\ 0 \cdot 93 \times \text{size} = \text{constant}.$$

Subsequent studies have shown that Pareto's law of income distribution is similar to the rank–size rule.

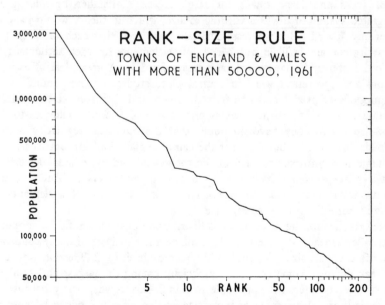

FIG. 8. Rank–size of towns of England and Wales with more than 50,000 inhabitants, 1961.

A number of scholars have noted the empirical relationships, others have made mathematical contributions, but it was Zipf who most publicized the rank–size rule, attempting to explain the relationships in a general theory of human behaviour. His explanation involved two forces, those of *diversification* and *unification*. The former tends to split a population into small autarchic communities as a result of economical location near raw materials. Diversification tendencies minimize the problems of transportation of raw materials to factories, while unification tendencies minimize difficulties of transportation of manufactured goods. When both forces are operating, optimum population distribution with reference to these forces is said to occur. The rule has not gained universal acceptance. Rosing has claimed that the rank–size rule is meaningless by itself, as it is only a special case of skewed distribution. Testing by chi-square the five largest cities of 132 countries, he obtained results which indicated that the rank–size rule was an inadequate description in all cases. But the rule must be seen in conjunction with central place theory.

The German, Christaller, conceiving a town as a central place within a rural area, and, later, his compatriot Lösch, both assumed a functional size-class hierarchy of towns as a basis of analysis of their spatial arrangement, function and size. The basic assumptions are that a rural area supports a town which in turn serves the rural area, and that there are small towns for small areas and large towns for large areas. Christaller postulated an integrated system of towns according to size, which in theory would have to be evenly spaced. But whereas Christaller assumed that each order in the hierarchy contains a fixed number, k, of settlements for each settlement of the order above, Lösch does not assume a fixed k. A great deal of experimental and theoretical work in central place studies revolves round these assumptions of fixed k and non-fixed k. Berry and Garrison see the general location theories of urban places as one of several alternate schemes to the rank–size rule. They have no doubt that the empirical regularity in the rank–size rule exists, but feel that the causal explanations are not clear.

Bunge has synthesized much of the theoretical and experimental work in central place theory which has often led to controversy. Much of the controversy is concerned with whether there is a hierarchy of settlements or a continuum of variously sized places.

Stewart favours the discontinuous distribution of town sizes, and supports Christaller's idea of the fixed k. He made detailed analyses of many countries to verify the rank–size rule, but found no logical basis in it. The rule was seen to break down in some countries, especially among the largest and smallest towns. He considered it applicable to middle-size towns, partly because of the variety of determinants of town size and spacing and partly because of "the gross coincidence of the rank–size rule and the town-function pyramid".

Stewart also found the rule more accurate for large heterogeneous areas than small homogeneous ones, where town size, functions and spacing are closely connected.

Furthermore, Stewart found no evidence to support the theory of a hierarchy of urban centres, nothing "natural" about the shape of the town-size pyramid. He found that the relative sizes and numbers of towns in different functional classes (the value of k) vary according to the level of economic development. Standard of living was considered the best index of determinants of k, a rise in standard of living tending to reduce the value of k, to increase the difference in population of towns in different function classes, and to shift more functions to larger towns. Consequently, areas with large urban structures tend to have S-shaped town-size distributions rather than linear logarithmic distributions.

Berry rejected the hypothesis that the progression from a concentration in a primate city to a rank–size distribution is a function of the level of economic development of countries and found that it resulted from the ageing and growing complexity of urban society.

Browning and Gibbs have demonstrated a way of expressing rank–size relationship and deviations from it by calculating both the number of places and the populations which would be anticipated for various size-classes and by comparing them with the actual distribution. They also compared conformity to the rank–size rule in the same countries at different times to assess the stability of the rank–size hierarchy.

Large Cities

The growth of large cities is just as remarkable as the general process of urbanization. They now include more than one-fifth of the world's population. But what is a large city? A simple definition by size uses the lower level of 100,000 inhabitants, but should we consider the city proper, or its agglomeration? In any case, what is an agglomeration? By this term many Americans mean the fusion of two cities to form one unit, whereas in France an agglomeration is a city with its suburbs. The United Nations *Demographic Yearbook* defines an urban agglomeration "as including the suburban fringe or thickly settled territory lying outside of, but adjacent to, the city boundaries".

The growth of large agglomerations often leads to the formation of composite urban settlements, interconnected and interdependent, now commonly called conurbations. As Freeman has so ably demonstrated, the term "conurbation" has had various connotations, although it might be simply described as an assemblage or continuum of towns, sometimes composed of a single large agglomeration and its satellite towns. Conurbations are never easy to study, demographically, geographically or otherwise. Even more difficult are urbanized regions or metropolitan communities, which comprise assemblages of conurbations and towns. Studies of individual cases are much easier than comparative studies, and the latter are extremely problematical on an international level.

In general, the proportion living in large cities is highest in industrialized countries and lowest in agricultural countries, although the correlation is not always clear, as we see from the numerous large cities in Indonesia, Mexico, and Colombia. Moreover, it should not be construed from the above remarks that large cities are not important in low latitudes. Indeed, a large proportion of the urban population of Africa, South America and South-East Asia lives in large cities, especially "millionaire" cities. Capitals of African and South American countries are containing an increasing share of the urban populations. Administrative, commercial and port functions accelerate the growth of such cities as Buenos Aires, Montevideo, Tunis, Dakar, Conakry, Freetown, Abidjan, Lagos and Dar es Salaam. European countries are not spared this over-concentration in primate cities; Paris, Vienna, Stockholm and Copenhagen all hold substantial proportions of their country's town-dwellers.

Urban primacy may be determined by a two-city index $\left(\dfrac{P_1}{P_2}\right)$, or a four-city index $\left(\dfrac{P_1}{P_2 + P_3 + P_4}\right)$, but the latter is more independent of the total number of cities.

A high degree of primacy, as in Mexico, Argentina and Uruguay, usually means low conformity to the rank–size rule. High urban primacy tends to occur in countries with small areas of dense population, low *per capita* income, export-orientated and agricultural economies, a colonial past and rapid population growth.

Millionaire cities are multiplying rapidly. At the beginning of this century there were only eleven in the world; in the early 1960s there were more than 100. In his study of these mammoth cities, Linton emphasized the rise in average size, the growing proportion of the world's population living in them, the southward shift of the mean latitude of millionaire cities, and their recent rapid growth in the tropics. Even little-urbanized Africa now has six (Cairo, Alexandria, Casablanca, Lagos, Kinshasa and Johannesburg), while South America has nine (Buenos Aires, Rio de Janeiro, Sao Paulo, Santiago, Bogota, Caracas, Recife, Belo Horizonte, and Lima). Nevertheless, there are still only nine millionaire cities in the southern hemisphere.

The absolute size of large cities is also increasing quickly, and many agglomerations of tens of millions must be expected. Davis has suggested that by A.D. 2000 the largest city in India may have between 36 and 66 million people, and the second between 18 and 33 millions.

These considerations inevitably lead us to the question of optimum size, an important matter for countries faced with high urban primacy at the expense of stagnating or slowly growing medium-sized towns. Some have suggested that the maximum size of a city should be 50,000 inhabitants, for reasons of health, public safety and physical plan. But these criteria are not indicative of optimum size for municipal efficiency, traffic flow, family and group life, social contentment, cultural innovations, or for educational, recreational and retail facilities. In fact, a variety of sizes answer to optimum conditions for different criteria. In any case, it looks as if we shall have to get used to facing the problems of growing urban size.

Urban Population Densities

Studies in the United States have shown a rather consistent relationship between city size, measured on a logarithmic scale, and average density of population, whether the latter is measured for the total area or the built-up area.

The spatial patterns of cities, their division into central business districts, industrial quarters, divers residential areas and transitional zones, have induced urban geographers to theorize about the location of these various zones and quarters. The theories do not concern us here, but it is obvious that the disposition of the quarters greatly influences population distribution within a city. Indeed, the contrasts in population density between a central business district, a high-class housing area, and a tenement quarter are much greater than can be found in most rural districts.

Although any particular city may have an irregular distribution of population within its confines, cities in general tend to conform to common patterns of internal population distribution. In a study of this subject, Clark begins with two "universally recognized" assumptions:

"1. In every large city, excluding the central business zone, which has few resident inhabitants, we have districts of dense population in the interior, with density falling off progressively as we proceed to the outer suburbs.

2. In most (but not all) cities, as time goes on, density tends to fall in the most populous inner suburbs, and to rise in the outer suburbs, and the whole city tends to spread itself out."

He then proceeded to show that for all cities studied, the decline in population density towards the outer suburb follows a simple mathematical equation of exponential decline:

$$y = Ae^{-bx}$$

where x is the distance in miles from the centre of the city; y is the density

of resident population in thousands per square mile; b is a coefficient
measuring the rate of decline of density; and A is a coefficient measuring
the degree of overcrowding in the centre of the city.

In 36 cities average densities were calculated for concentric rings (one mile
in width) about the centre, assuming no central business district and a
uniform spread, although Clark acknowledged that it would be better to use
census tracts (or enumeration districts) than concentric rings. Both coefficients
are mathematically related to the total population of the city, and may be
determined by using a diagram in which the horizontal coordinate is the
distance in miles from the centre of the city to the mid-point of the concentric
ring under examination, and the vertical coordinate is the natural logarithm
of the density in thousands per square mile. Data tend to form a straight
line, except for the central business district. The value of the coefficient A is
obtained from the point at which the line cuts the vertical axis, and the value
of b from its slope; both values of A and b vary from city to city. High values
were typical of early nineteenth-century London and Paris; much lower values
of b are recorded by most twentieth-century cities (see Fig. 9). Among the
more surprising points of Clark's study was the fact that the difference in
dispersal between such cities as Manchester and Los Angeles is surprisingly
small.

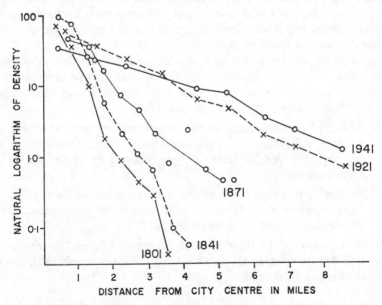

FIG. 9. Density gradients for London at various dates, 1801–1941. After
CLARK, C., Urban population densities, *J.R. Stat. Soc.*, Ser. A, **114**, 490 (1951).

By studying cities of the United States and Britain, Stewart and Warntz came to a similar conclusion on the exponential decline of density radially from the peak in all directions. They found that on the average the area of a city is proportional to the three-fourths power of its total population, and that the central density depends on the size of population (see Fig. 10). "As population increases the increased 'attraction' (demographic gravitation) between people weighs down on and compresses the central population." They demonstrated also that, in areas where general potential of population is low, cities tend to have larger areas than cities of similar size in areas of high population potential. Newling has postulated that since both urban population densities and the growth rate are functions of distance from the city centre, then one can arrive at a population density-growth rule, which states that urban population densities at the beginning of a given period and the associated rates of population change are inversely related.

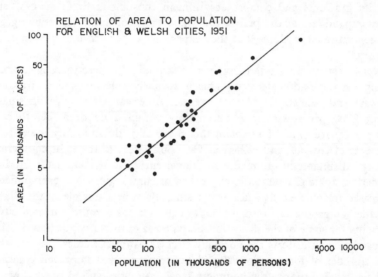

FIG. 10. The relation of area to population for English and Welsh towns with more than 50,000 inhabitants, 1951. The 20 largest cities are shown individually, the next 40 by medians of groups of 5, and the following 50 by medians of groups of 10. Following are two groups of 15 and one of 17. The line indicates that the area of a town varies directly as the three-fourths power of the population. After STEWART, J. Q. and WARNTZ, W., *op. cit.*

Subsequent studies of population densities of cities all over the world support Clark's argument, with varying degrees of significance. Berry, Simmons and Tennant provide a theoretical rationale for Clark's formula by stating that the negative exponential decline of densities is a logical outcome of urban-land-use theory. They note that the most desirable sites in Western cities are central, where net returns and prices of land are highest. As these diminish outwards, declining residential densities should be expected. In Western cities the poor are concentrated near the city centre and the rich are dispersed near the periphery. Muth postulates that the negative exponential decline of densities results from a negative exponential price–distance relationship. He shows how in large cities of the United States price per unit of housing, rent per unit of land, and output of housing per unit of land all decline with distance from the city centre, while *per capita* consumption of housing increases outwards.

Berry, Simmons and Tennant claim that density gradient and degrees of compactness diminish as city size increases, and that density gradient is also a function of the distortion of the city shape and the proportion of manufacturing outside the central city. As Western cities grow they experience suburban sprawl. This is not true for many non-Western cities, where density gradients and compactness remain constant in time. Non-Western cities expand less at the periphery, where the poor and least mobile groups are concentrated in slums, but they experience continued increases in central density.

Non-Western cities often have very sharp edges, where there is an abrupt change in population density. This is specially true for walled cities. But Stewart and Warntz found that even in American cities edge densities of about 2000 per square mile fell rapidly within a hundred feet to below 200 per square mile. To explain this sharp edge density, they resort to the concepts of *cohesion* and *adhesion*. Cohesion refers to the joint co-operation of city inhabitants in producing additional energy to that normally produced by demographic gravitation in any urban or rural region; it is exemplified by increased telephone calls and motor traffic. By adhesion is meant the clinging together of people to desirable land, such as a main route out of a city; it accounts for some of the distortions in patterns of urban population densities. In particular, it distorts the normally circular pattern of cities.

A number of forces, especially motor transport and improved communications, tend to reduce the boundary tension of cities and to break down the high edge densities. Ribbon development has assisted this process. In many cases the edge density has diminished so much that it is difficult to determine the limits of town and country. The declining significance of high edge densities of towns is one of the most important aspects of the population geography of the twentieth century.

In this century we have seen the growing distinction between the "residential city" and the "occupational city"; the spatial distributions of people in their dwellings and at their jobs were formerly much more coincident than nowadays. Stewart and Warntz stress that, owing to the interplay of various economies achieved by the concentration or dispersal of places of employment, the lowering of the city's edge density for industry is even more pronounced than for dwellings. But this is less the result of massive industrial decentralization than of decongestion of dense industrial belts and proliferation of light industries in suburban sprawls.

Rural Population Categories

The term "rural population" has been defined in various ways, and even sociologists cannot agree as to a definition, but the population geographer must usually accept as rural anything which is not officially classified as urban. Inevitably, this means that much officially rural population is actually urban in function and location.

Several elements should be taken into account by the geographer when considering rurality. The first is population density, but the problem is in deciding on a suitable threshold, below which populations may be considered rural. The second element is function or occupation, and here the difficulty is which to include of the four groups of primary population—agriculturalists, forestry workers, fishermen and miners. Generally, the last two are excluded and only agricultural, forestry and associated service populations are considered as truly rural. The third element is land use, and it has been held by some authors that, in view of the decline of rural populations in developed countries and the growth of non-primary populations in rural areas, extensive land use can provide a better definition of rurality than either density or function. The fourth element is situation, particularly in relation to urban centres, which have a considerable influence upon rural populations. All these elements may be incorporated into a statistical analysis of rural populations.

Rural population includes three distinct functional elements — basic (or primary), secondary and adventitious. The basic rural population is directly dependent upon the land or sea, and includes those engaged in agriculture, forestry and fishing. Miners and quarrymen have also been put into this category, but many are urban dwellers. Secondary rural population serves the needs of the primary population: shopkeepers, professional men, officials, transport workers, etc. The adventitious rural population lives in the country by choice, but is not engaged in basic or secondary activities; it is residential, dormitory or defence population and is usually growing in importance.

In a stable society a numerical balance tends to arise between the basic and secondary rural populations. Using only two categories of primary and secondary rural population, Stevens found that in lowland parts of England and Wales the whole rural population was about double the primary rural population. Vince, however, using three categories, suggested that the secondary rural population was about half the primary. The ratio of secondary to primary rural population varies regionally according to physical features, types of farming, settlement patterns and accessibility.

Robertson has examined the relationships of the three categories of rural population in England and Wales, and concludes that Rural Districts comprise three distinct types of population — agricultural–rural, rural and rural–urban. Agricultural–rural populations are usually located in less accessible areas, where agriculturalists represent over half of the occupational structure, and where the adventitious population is small. Among typical rural populations, the basic rural population accounts for about 45 per cent of the total, the secondary population about 50 per cent, and the adventitious population about 5 per cent. Much more extensive is the rural–urban belt, where less than one-third of the population are engaged in agricultural pursuits and where the adventitious population accounts for more than one-quarter. The rural–urban belt may be divided into seven types of district: defence, suburban (residential, dormitory and industrial), mining–rural, manufacturing–rural and mining–manufacturing Rural Districts. Robertson notes that three-quarters of the Rural Districts in England and Wales are rural–urban, a further indication of the inadequacy of the census definition of rural population.

One great difficulty is that both secondary and adventitious components of rural population include a great variety of occupational and industrial groupings. As Vince has said: "The exact size of a secondary population in an area cannot therefore be read off from a census table. It is an absolute concept, and may not be even composed of whole individuals! The sum total of what are usually termed the 'service trades' . . . is manifestly no guide whatever to the size of the secondary population, because these service trades serve the whole community and not specifically the primary element." Moreover, much of the population serving the primary rural population is located in towns ("town secondary population").

The heterogeneity of the rural population is a common phenomenon in advanced economies. In the United States, Zelinsky has noted at least seven categories of what is termed the "rural-nonfarm" population: "(1) essentially urban persons who live in villages or unincorporated segments of the urban fringes of cities of fewer than 50,000 people; (2) retired persons and persons working in cities who live in dispersed rural dwellings; (3) residents of agglomerated settlements (hamlets and villages) in rural territory beyond urbanized areas; (4) dispersed rural folk engaged in nonagricultural but distinctly rural activities (for example, forestry, mining, fishing, trapping, and various services for rural residents); (5) dispersed rural folk employed in transportation, recreational services, highway services, and other occupations catering to transients and seasonal visitors; (6) institutional populations and military personnel stationed at rural camps; (7) students living on rural campuses or in rural residences while attending college." But in the absence of differentiated data, it is difficult to examine these elements separately.

Rural Population Patterns

Rural population patterns are dependent upon patterns of rural settlement. Despite the accepted terminology of nucleated and dispersed settlement patterns, there is a wide gamut of patterns from the highly dispersed to the highly concentrated. Furthermore, there is a complete range of settlement sizes from the isolated house to the town, between which extremes it is difficult to allocate the terms hamlet and village. Figures of 10 and 100 inhabitants have been suggested for distinguishing between isolated buildings, hamlets and villages, but no population figures can adequately perform this function. The distinction reflects more the organization of communal life.

A number of statistical methods have been devised for analysing the degree of dispersion and concentration of rural settlement. Most do not incorporate population data, but are concerned only with the density of settlements or housing. However, with French population data, which give for each commune the population of the chief place and the population of the rest of the commune, Demangeon was able to suggest the following coefficient of dispersion:

$$C = \frac{E \times N}{T}$$

where E is the population of those settlements outside of the commune centre, N is the number of settlements, and T is the total population of the commune.

As an index of nucleation, the Northumberland County Council divided the population of settlements of 20 inhabitants or more by the dispersed population, in order to demonstrate that parishes with a high degree of nucleation tend to be more stable in population total.

Detailed population maps of rural areas are largely based on settlement traces, and analysis of the influences upon the patterns involves the same considerations of relief, soils, water-supply, ethnic and agricultural traditions, defensive needs and evolutionary processes.

References

BERRY, B. J. L., The impact of expanding metropolitan communities upon the central place hierarchy, *Ann. Assoc. Amer. Geographers*, **50**, 112 (1960).

BERRY, B. J. L., City size distributions and economic development, *Econ. Development and Cultural Change*, **9**, 573 (1961).

BERRY, B. J. L. and GARRISON, W. L., Alternate explanations of rank–size relationships, *Ann. Assoc. Amer. Geographers*, **48**, 83 (1958).

BERRY, B. J. L., SIMMONS, J. W. and TENNANT, R. J., Urban population densities: structure and change, *Geog. Review*, **53**, 389 (1963).

BRACEY, H. E., *People and the Countryside*, 1970.

BUNGE, W., *Theoretical Geography*, Lund, 1962.

CLARK, C., Urban population densities, *J.R. Stat. Soc.*, Ser. A, **114**, 490 (1951).
CLARK, C., Urban population densities, *Bull. Inst. International de Statistique*, **36**, 60 (1958).
DAVIS, K., *World Urbanization 1950–70*, Berkeley, 1969.
DICKINSON, R. E., *City and Region*, 1964.
FREEMAN, T. W., *The Conurbations of Britain*, 1959.
GEORGE, P., *Précis de géographie urbaine*, 1961.
GIBBS, J. P., The evolution of population concentration, *Econ. Geog.*, **39**, 119 (1963).
GIBBS, J. P. (Ed.), *Urban Research Methods*, Princeton, 1961.
GIBBS, J. P., Measures of urbanization, *Social Forces*, **45**, 170 (1966).
HAUSER, P. M. and SCHORE, L. F. (Eds.), *The Study of Urbanization*, New York, 1965.
ISARD, W., *Location and Space-Economy*, Glencoe, Ill., 1957.
JOHNSON, J. H., *Urban Geography: An Introductory Analysis*, 1967.
KAMERSCHEN, D. R., Further analysis of overurbanization, *Econ. Development and Cultural Change*, **17**, 235 (1969).
LINSKY, A., Some generalisations concerning primate cities, *Ann. Assoc. Amer. Geographers*, **55**, 506 (1965).
LINTON, D. L., Millionaire cities to-day and yesterday, *Geography*, **43**, 253 (1958).
MAYER, H. M. and KOHN, C. F. (Eds.), *Readings in Urban Geography*, Glencoe, Ill., 1959.
MOUNTJOY, A. B., Million cities: urbanization and developing countries, *Geography*, **53**, 365 (1968).
NEWLING, B. E., The spatial variation of urban population densities, *Geog. Review*, **59**, 242 (1969).
NORBORG, K., *Proceedings of I.G.U. Symposium on Urban Studies*, Lund Studies in Geography, Ser. B, Human Geography, No. 24, 1962.
ROBERTSON, I. M. L., The occupational structure and distribution of rural population in England and Wales, *Scot. Geog. Mag.*, **77**, 165 (1961).
ROSING, K. E., A rejection of the Zipf model (rank size rule) in relation to city size, *Professional Geographer*, **18**, 75 (1966).
SOVANI, N. V., The analysis of overurbanization, *Econ. Development and Cultural Change*, **72**, 113 (1964).
STEVENS A., The distribution of rural population in Great Britain, *Trans. Inst. Brit. Geogr.*, **11**, 23 (1946).
STEWART, C. T., The size and spacing of cities, *Geog. Review*, **48**, 222 (1958).
STEWART, J. Q., Urban population densities, *Geog. Review*, **43**, 575 (1953).
STEWART, J. Q. and WARNTZ, W., Physics of population distribution, *J. Regional Science*, **1**, 99 (1958).
U.N., *Demographic Yearbook*, 1962.
VINCE, S. W. E., Reflections on the structure and distribution of rural population in England and Wales, 1921–1931, *Trans. Inst. Brit. Geogr.*, **18**, 53 (1952).
ZELINSKY, W., Changes in the geographic patterns of rural population in the United States, 1790–1960, *Geog. Review*, **52**, 492 (1962).
ZIPF, G. K., *Human Behaviour and the Principle of Least Effort*, Cambridge, Mass., 1949.

CHAPTER VI

PATTERNS OF POPULATION COMPOSITION

So FAR in this book we have largely ignored the individuality of human beings and the diversity of communities; we have treated man as a unit. We realize, however, that the population of the world is so varied physically, socially, economically, and politically that satisfactory classification is almost impossible. The problem has been further aggravated by varied definitions and connotations of terms like marriage, divorce, family, household, industry, nationality, language, religion, race, class, culture. Data are therefore variable, and international comparability low. Another difficulty is that of isolating any particular aspect of population; how can one consider size of families without an examination of age-structure, and how can one understand social class without study of occupation and income?

Population Composition

The composition of the population, or the population structure, refers to those aspects of population which may be measured, however inadequately. But we must restrict ourselves to aspects for which data are usually obtained from censuses: age, sex, marital status, the size and composition of families and households, economic activities, nationality, language and religion. These are sometimes termed the quantitative aspects, in contrast to qualitative aspects such as physical and psychological characteristics and social and cultural groupings. It is also possible to distinguish between those aspects which are innate (sex, age, race) and those which are acquired during life (marriage, family, occupation), as well as between those which are individual and those which are communal.

Geographers are interested in population structure as it varies territorially between countries, regions, urban and rural areas, communities and ethnic groups. Unfortunately, studies in regional geography have too often either neglected population structure or have treated only some aspects, such as language and religion. Yet sex and age-composition and the size of families may have even more striking effects upon housing, educational and medical facilities, motor traffic, and many other features of the cultural landscape.

No study of rural Britain, for example, can neglect to mention the shortage of young women and children and its effects upon community life. No study of African towns can ignore the excess of young men. Geographers should not deal with population numbers alone; they must also consider population composition.

1. AGE-STRUCTURE

The study of age-structure (sometimes termed age-composition or age-distribution) has been too often neglected by geographers, perhaps because it is less easily observed and appreciated than some other aspects of the composition of population. Too often statements are made about population growth in absolute numbers without reference to changes in age-structure, yet one cannot proceed very far in the study of population growth or migration without examination of age-structure. Moreover, there is hardly an aspect of individual or communal life which is not affected by age: economic and social activities, military service, political propensities, social attitudes, mobility. . . . Furthermore, age-structure is directly influenced by three variables: mortality, fertility and migrations. These variables are not entirely independent, and any change in one may eventually influence the other two, but social and economic conditions only influence age-structure through them.

Although age is the aspect of population composition most commonly investigated in enumerations, it is also one plagued by mis-statements due to ignorance, carelessness or misrepresentation. Consequently, returns for even ages are often larger than those for odd ages, returns for females less accurate than those for males, and omissions of young children frequent. Fortunately, statisticians have several methods for determining the accuracy of age returns.

Age data are often presented in several different ways: age-groups, indices, pyramids and divergence graphs.

Age-groups

The average age of a cricket eleven or a boat crew is meaningful because the age-scatter is usually small, but the average age of a large population with a wide scatter is far less significant as it indicates very little about that scatter. Therefore, the population is usually divided into age-groups, quinquennially, decennially or into just three groups for which data may be presented as absolute numbers or as percentages of the total population:

(a) *Infants and Adolescents:* 0–14 or 0–19 years. This group is largely non-reproductive and increasingly non-productive, especially in modern societies, where there has been a marked tendency for the proportion in this age-group to diminish.

(b) *Adults:* 15–59, 15–64, 19–59 or 19–64 years, the age range depending partly on the age-composition. The adult age-group is the most reproductive and productive and supports the bulk of the other two groups. It is also the most mobile age-group. In advanced countries with low fertility and mortality, there has been little increase in the proportion of adults because the growing proportion of old persons is largely compensated by the diminishing proportion of children. From the point of view of production, the ratio of this age-group to the rest of the population should be high, as in Europe and immigrant countries. The adult age-group is sometimes subdivided for further analysis into young adults (e.g. 15–34) and older adults (e.g. 35–64).

(c) *The Aged:* 60 and over, or 65 and over. Except in some developing countries, this group includes a marked majority of females, who are mostly non-productive and include a high proportion of widows. Old men are usually more productive and may be reproductive. The proportion of the aged to the total population tends to increase as the population evolves.

The social and economic implications of these three age-groups and the geographical variations in their distribution are worthy of serious consideration. The first and third groups are more or less dependent on the second, and so close attention should be given to any measures which may affect the length of active life, especially delays in the commencement of active life due to prolonged education and changes in the age of retirement.

The proportion of the adult population does not vary greatly from country to country, but is generally inversely related to the levels of fertility and mortality, except where migration causes distortion. The main regional differences are in the proportions of children and old people, which tend to be in inverse relationship. The proportion of children, sometimes called *juvenility*, is below one-quarter in parts of western Europe due to low fertility, and thus contrasts greatly with high fertility developing countries of Africa, Latin America and Asia, where over 40 per cent of the population are under 15. On the other hand, such populations have high mortality and thus very few old people (Fig. 11). Indeed, the vast majority of world populations are heavily weighted in the young and adult age-groups, and the number of countries with a high proportion of old people are few and largely restricted to Europe. This situation is, however, quite recent. Figure 12 shows the changes in the proportions of four age-groups in Great Britain between 1851 and 1961. The obvious features are the continual increase in the proportion of old people between 1891 and 1951, the continual decline of young people between 1881 and the last war, and the change during the 1950s resultin from higher birth rates.

Population Geography

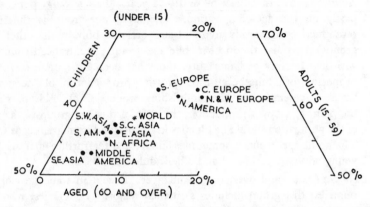

FIG. 11. Triangular graph of three age-groups in various regions of the world, 1945–54. This type of graph may be used for showing intercensal changes in one country.

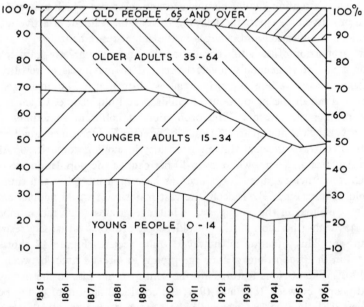

FIG. 12. The changing proportions of four age-groups in Great Britain between 1851 and 1961.

Age-indices

A clearer picture of the relationships of the three age-groups may sometimes be gained by calculating and mapping age-indices, each of which is expressed as a percentage:

(a) $\dfrac{\text{Children}}{\text{Adults}}$ (b) $\dfrac{\text{Children}}{\text{Aged}}$ (c) $\dfrac{\text{Children}}{\text{Adults} + \text{Aged}}$

(d) $\dfrac{\text{Aged}}{\text{Children} + \text{Adults}}$ (e) $\dfrac{\text{Children} + \text{Aged}}{\text{Adults}}$ (f) $\dfrac{\text{Aged}}{\text{Adults}}$

(g) $\dfrac{\text{Aged}}{\text{Children}}$

Among the most common are (f) known as the *old-age index,* and (e) the *dependency ratio.*

Age-pyramids

Age-groups and age-indices are generalizations. More detailed analysis of age-structure is possible by the construction of age-pyramids. The vertical axis is graduated in years or groups of years from 0 upwards, and the horizontal axes show either the numbers or the percentages of males and females within these groups; in practice, the percentage method is better for comparison of pyramids, but sometimes percentages are calculated of sexes separately and sometimes of the total population, and these result in differing pyramids. Naturally, pyramids are most revealing when the vertical steps are in years, but frequently they are presented in 5-year groups.

In particular, the age-pyramid is valuable in demonstrating the sex differential in age-structure, although this may be seen more clearly when both sexes are plotted on the same axis in the form of two profiles. An age-pyramid is rarely symmetrical, for, as we shall see in the next section, the sex-ratio differs from age to age. The preponderance of women in the older age-groups is usually clearly revealed in the age-pyramid.

The word pyramid is only really appropriate for graphs of populations with a high proportion in the younger age-groups, but this still applies to the majority of world populations. In advanced communities age-pyramids have more varied and more complex forms. Certain basic types of pyramid may be distinguished. First, if a population has unchanging fertility and mortality it is a stationary population, and each step in the pyramid will differ from the one below only by the number of deaths at that age or age-group. If, however, the number of births increases from year to year, the population type will become *progressive,* and the pyramid will widen at the base; decline in the number of births will produce a *regressive* population with a pyramid which is narrow at the base and has the shape of a bell. Figure 13 presents six examples of contrasting age-pyramids at mid-century, ranging from that of

Brazil which is very progressive to that of France which is regressive. The former is typical of a host of countries with high fertility and high or diminishing mortality, and the latter is typical of western Europe, where both fertility and mortality are low. Of course, in the nineteenth century most west European countries had progressive pyramids.

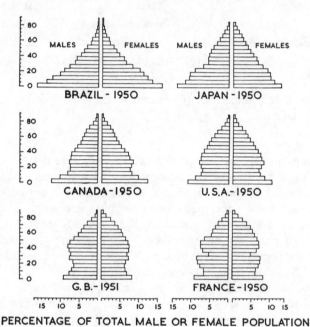

PERCENTAGE OF TOTAL MALE OR FEMALE POPULATION
AGES ARE IN FIVE-YEAR GROUPS

FIG. 13. Six age-pyramids at mid-century, contrasting young and old populations. The population pyramid of Great Britain in 1851 was not unlike that of Japan in 1950.

Age-pyramids not only reflect long-term trends in fertility and mortality, they are also sensitive to the short-term effects of wars, migrations, epidemics, "baby-booms", population policies and other phenomena, and with practice one can interpret both the shape and the many irregularities in age-pyramids. On occasions they can be usefully mapped to show regional differences.

Unfortunately, it is not easy to compare a mass of age-pyramids, and faced with this difficulty Coulson devised an age-structure index, which is the angle of slope of a generalized age-structure histogram. Like other age indices, it obscures the details of age–sex structure but may be mapped and used for further statistical analysis; unlike them, it is not immediately comprehensible.

Ageing of Population

The term "ageing of population" lacks precision. Does it mean a larger proportion of aged persons, or a smaller proportion of young persons? It has been suggested that the former trend should be termed "ageing at the apex" and the latter "ageing at the base". In economically advanced countries with low fertility both of these trends have been apparent, and as countries with high fertility and declining mortality have a remarkably stable age-structure it must be inferred that changes in fertility have played a more important role in ageing than have changes in mortality. One reason, perhaps, is that the decline in mortality in underdeveloped countries has initially affected only the younger age-groups, without any accompanying decline in fertility, and consequently there is rejuvenation at the base but no change at the apex. However, mortality and fertility are independent only to a certain extent; mortality cannot decline indefinitely without affecting fertility at some point through a reduction in the size of families, because of the heavy burden of children on the remainder of the population. In such countries there are prospects of considerable ageing at the apex as well as at the base, as in Japan today.

In advanced countries mortality has reached very low levels among the lower age-groups, and as further medical progress will undoubtedly reduce the afflictions of adult life and old-age, one can reasonably assume continued increase in the numbers of old people. It is true that these countries have experienced a slowing-down or cessation in the decline of fertility or even some revival, and that this will cause some reduction in ageing, but the effects of the major decline in fertility are still with us. The number of old people in the advanced countries is likely to increase. It is estimated that the number of people aged 65 and over in the United Kingdom will almost certainly increase rapidly until the 1980s, and that without the higher fertility of post-war years we would have had probably the highest proportion of old people in the world (Fig. 14). In the near future, we can also count on a continued increase in the proportion of older adults. Several other European countries are experiencing similar trends, notably Belgium, Austria and Sweden. The rate of increase in the proportion of old people is also striking in the U.S.A., Australia and New Zealand, and already the proportion exceeds that prevailing in the countries of southern Europe.

The social and economic implications of ageing are widespread, and have caused some alarm. We should not forget that demographic ageing is the sum of individual ageing which in turn is the sum of physiological and intellectual ageing, which occur at different rates in different people. The economic activity of the population is only one aspect of the effects of ageing. Consumption also changes with ageing; requirements of foodstuffs, housing, schools, hospitals, transport, pensions and so on. The aged in advanced

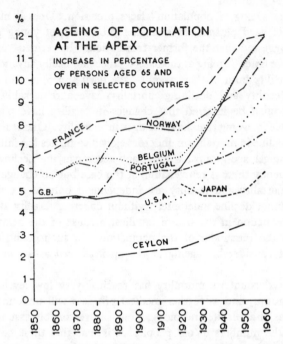

FIG. 14. Ageing of population at the apex in selected countries, especially in western Europe. Few Commonwealth countries are faced with this problem, although in Australia and New Zealand about 8·5 per cent are aged 65 and over.

societies are specialized consumers, but are not usually producers, and consequently must rely on their families, their savings or their countries. The family has largely lost this function, but neither savings nor the state have satisfactorily replaced it.

Differential Age-structure

So far we have confined our attention to the age-structure of countries, but of course there are great differences in age-structure within countries, especially those which are heterogeneous ethnically, economically and socially.

Ethnic groups with different degrees of economic and social developments have different demographic habits and accordingly different age-structures. The European and Maori populations of New Zealand form an excellent example; although the Maoris now constitute only about 8 per cent of the total population, they are a very youthful people and this proportion is growing annually. They are, however, essentially rural and localized in the northern half of North Island, so the problems associated with their growth are limited to a few areas. In the Republics of South Africa and Zambia and in Rhodesia similar contrasts exist between the Europeans and Africans, and in the United States between the negroes and whites. But disparity also occurs between less-contrasted ethnic groups, as we see in the United States and Canada where the various immigrant groups have diverse age-structures. The French-Canadian population, for example, is younger overall than the English-speaking Canadian population.

Age-compositions of rural and urban populations usually differ considerably, due not only to different fertility and mortality trends, but also to the effects of migrations. In most Western countries, at least, fertility tends to be lower in towns (except new towns) than in the country and consequently urban populations have fewer children than rural populations. Until recently mortality has also been much lower in the country than in towns, and therefore rural populations have tended to have more old people than urban populations; but in Britain, the United States and several other countries there has been a rapid decline in urban mortality in recent years, so some towns have more old people than have surrounding rural areas.

Migrations to and from towns continually modify their age-structure, because they mainly involve young adults, whose loss to rural areas increases the proportion of old people and eventually reduces the number of children. This situation is sometimes aggravated by a movement of old people from the town to the country on retirement. The general effects of all these tendencies can be seen in Fig. 15, which shows the remarkable changes in the age and sex-structures of rural districts in England and Wales between 1911 and 1951. Franklin constructed a whole series of such diagrams to demonstrate the diverse age-structures of communities in the North Island of New Zealand. In African, Asian and Latin American towns the proportion of young adults is especially high, causing unbalanced population structure.

There is a danger of over-generalization. All towns do not have a high proportion of young adults. One should not expect Bath to have the same age-structure as Bristol, or Nice as Nancy. Seaside resorts and spas in Britain are specially attractive to old people on retirement, and have old populations. Also, many small market towns lose their young men to the larger cities and are hence similarly weighted at the apex. Furthermore, within any particular town there are wide differences in age-composition, as we see in the various phases of housing development in any large suburban area of Britain. Scott, Coulson and Rochefort have all noted that the aged tend to live in the older and more central quarters of urban agglomerations, while the young live in newer suburbs, but obviously there are exceptions, as in wealthier suburbs where the aged are more common.

Rural areas have also been variously affected by depopulation of young people and the settlement of old people. Thus, rural areas in the south-west of England have a more aged population than have those of the south-east,

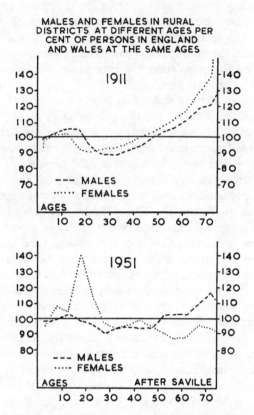

MALES AND FEMALES IN RURAL
DISTRICTS AT DIFFERENT AGES PER
CENT OF PERSONS IN ENGLAND
AND WALES AT THE SAME AGES

FIG. 15. Deviational graphs of percentage deviations of quinquennial age-groups from the national average (represented by straight lines) of males and females in rural districts of England and Wales, 1911 and 1951. After SAVILLE, J., *Rural Depopulation in England and Wales, 1851–1951,* 1957.

and similar contrasts may be drawn, for example, between the Massif Central of France and the Armorican Massif, and between the Rocky Mountain states of Montana and Idaho and their north-western neighbours Washington and Oregon.

Figure 16 reveals some of the striking regional differences in age-composition in England and Wales. The pattern is much more complex than in many other countries, owing to the congestion of population, the massive urban sprawls and the internal migration of both men and women. Nevertheless, in most countries the regional analysis of age-structure is well worth making, especially in relation to economic development and social provision.

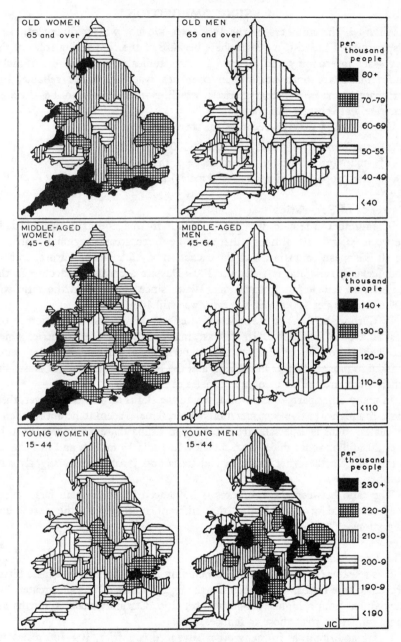

FIG. 16. The distribution of three age-groups of males and females in England and Wales by counties, 1951.

2. SEX-COMPOSITION

Although the numbers of the two sexes are not widely divergent, their disparity is of interest to geographers because of the contrasting roles of the two sexes in economy and society. Precise studies of the numbers of males and females are only possible in countries where data are reliable, but fortunately sex is the characteristic which is most likely to be declared accurately at census enumeration.

The sex-ratio may be recorded in three different ways:

(a) the number of males per 100 or 1000 females, or vice versa;
(b) males (or females) as a percentage of the total population;
(c) the proportion of males (or females) as a decimal of unity.

Patterns of Sex-ratios

The number of females per 100 males in individual countries varies usually between 90 and 110, although there may be much greater regional contrasts. In all European countries, with the exception of Albania, the Faroes, Ireland and Iceland, this ratio is well over 100. Despite a consistent decline in the majority of females in England and Wales since 1921, when the ratio was 109·6 females per 100 males, the ratio was still 106·6 in 1961.

In Europe, however, the sex-selective effects of war and emigration in the past have been formidable. In contrast, many of the overseas countries which received European immigrants still experience a surplus of males, most marked in pioneer fringes like Alaska and the Northern Territory of Australia, where there are half as many more males as females.

In many other parts of the world, where the status of women is lower, their mortality higher or their enumeration poorer, females seem to be outnumbered by males. This is especially true of Asia; in China there would appear to be over 20 million more males than females, in India 13 million and in Pakistan 5 million. On the other hand, in Indonesia and Japan females slightly outnumber males.

The ratio between the two sexes is influenced by three main factors: the preponderance of male births, the different mortality of the sexes, and migrations.

The Preponderance of Male Births

It is a feature of most mammals, including human beings, that male births exceed female births. At conception the excess of males is even greater, but they suffer from a higher pre-natal mortality. Certainly male stillbirths are more numerous than those of females.

In Great Britain, as in many other advanced countries, 104–106 males are born for every 100 females, and there has been an upward trend of male preponderance at birth since 1950. The causes of this trend are not certain, although there is reason to believe that the sex-ratio at birth is directly related to the standard of living and to the degree of pre-natal hygiene. In the United States, for example, male preponderance at birth is lower among negroes than among whites, and this may be the main reason for the majority of females in the negro population. On the other hand, race may be a significant factor. In fact, many factors have been believed to be associated with the human live birth sex-ratio, including maternal and paternal ages, ancestral longevity, war, cigarette smoking, coffee drinking and even baldness of the father, but some of these may now be discounted.

In some societies the desire for male children influences sex-ratios, and also the completion of a family on the achievement of a male child. In some cases this attitude leads to female infanticide, prevalent in many parts of Asia.

Different Mortality of the Sexes

Nearly all developed countries have higher male mortality than female mortality, and the disparity in the deaths of the two sexes is much greater than in the births. At birth males are therefore destined to a shorter life-span than are females.

The difference between male and female mortality is greatest in the United States. Canada, Argentina, Australia and the European population of New Zealand follow quite closely behind, but it is difficult to discern a significant world-wide pattern.

The more rapid decline of female mortality, influenced by environmental causes, seems largely due to biological factors. It appears that the gentler sex is also the stronger sex. Evidence of the relative weakness of males is their higher infant mortality, which rapidly reduces their initial numerical superiority. In most advanced countries mortality among males generally exceeds female mortality throughout life, so that women are particularly preponderant in the older age-groups. On the other hand, in several countries of Asia, Africa and Latin America high maternal mortality and sometimes the neglect of females raises young adult female mortality above that for males, and partly accounts for the overall excess of males.

Migrations and Sex–ratios

Migrations are sex-selective. In the past, men migrated more freely than women, but the increasing speed and efficiency of transportation has greatly facilitated female migration in advanced countries. The annual numbers of female migrants to and from the United Kingdom now usually exceed the numbers of males. We in Britain are rather exceptional in this respect, but the figures are symptomatic of a change in the character of European emigration which occurred in the inter-war years, especially the 1930s.

Population Geography

Until 1931, there was always a net loss of males by emigration from Great Britain as many of Britain's young men went Empire-building or to the New World. Many other European countries have similar tales to tell, and claim that their present female surpluses are due to the loss of "the flower of their youth" (a point of controversy) during the immense wave of trans-oceanic migrations in the nineteenth and early twentieth centuries. Italy is an obvious example. Most West Indian islands are in a similar position through recent emigration.

The great immigrant countries of this period all received more males than females, and by the First World War the male surplus in their populations was marked. There has since been an adjustment of the balance. At the beginning of this century there were 110 males in Australia for every 100 females; now the ratio is 101 : 100, the same as in Canada. In the hundred years before 1910 there were over half as many more male immigrants into the United States as females, and in that year there were 106 males for every 100 females. Now female immigrants clearly prevail and female mortality is much lower than that of males, so females form well over half of the total population. It is the same story in Brazil, and it may not be long before other old immigrant countries like Argentina retrieve a balance of the sexes.

Some small countries of recent immigration, like Israel, Taiwan, Kuwait and Hong Kong, have male surpluses, but the demographic futures of these territories are not easily predictable.

Internal migrations in advanced countries are also less sex-selective than in the past. Female migrants are becoming more and more numerous. In Britain the change to a preponderance of female migrants took place in the second half of the nineteenth century, and was noted as long ago as 1885 by E. G. Ravenstein in his classic paper on "The Laws of Migration". Women migrated to the towns to work in domestic service or in light industries, and came to form a high proportion of the urban population. Although female occupations have changed, the migration has continued, and so the country-side suffers from a dearth of women because of inadequate opportunities of employment. Saville explains that in rural districts there are fewer females than males in all age-groups from 4 to 49, and the effects on fertility as well as on social and economic life in rural areas have been drastic. Females are most prevalent in seaside and inland resorts, dormitory towns, market towns (especially in southern England and Wales), textile towns, and West London. The proportion of males is highest in military towns, ports, and in mining, engineering and chemical towns, and is generally higher near city centres than in suburbs. Consequently, there are strong regional differences in sex-ratios, as indicated in the map of England and Wales (Fig. 17).

In Australia and New Zealand females predominate in the towns, and they are more numerous in the relatively intensely farmed areas than in the

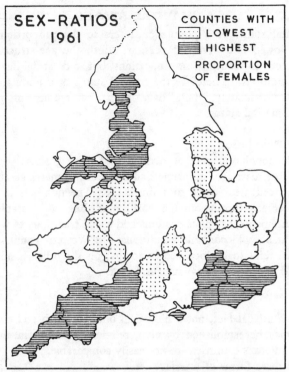

FIG. 17. The 15 counties in England and Wales with the highest sex-ratios and the 15 with the lowest, 1961. Sex-ratios range from 1252 females per 1000 males in East Sussex to 913 in Rutland.

isolated and sheep-farming areas. A similar pattern of sex-ratios may be found in the United States and Canada, but there is a general pattern of increasing male dominance towards the west — a relic feature perhaps of "Go west, young man".

In many developing countries men still form the bulk of the migrants. In towns of Africa and Asia (excluding the U.S.S.R., Japan and the Philippines) men are preponderant, especially in rapidly growing mining or industrial centres. In many Indian cities males have a crushing numerical superiority. A most notorious example is the Witwatersrand area of Johannesburg, where there are only 17 women per 100 men in the 15–45 age-group. In West African towns, the sex-ratios are much more balanced. Sometimes the sex-ratios of tribal groups within African towns seem to be influenced by the distance travelled to the town. The social and economic implications of male migrations are seen both in the tribal units, where cultivation often deteriorates and demographic fertility declines, and in the towns, where problems of assimilation of migrants are sometimes acute.

3. MARITAL STATUS

The marital status of a population refers to the proportions of single, married, widowed and divorced persons. Both the age-structure and the sex-ratio directly influence these proportions, but so do social institutions and economic conditions. Therefore the marital status of a population is never constant. Unfortunately, there have been few studies of geographical variations in marital status.

The Single Population

The single population may be divided into three groups: persons below the legal age of marriage, unmarried adults desiring marriage at some time or other, and celibates vowed to a single life. The numbers in these three groups vary greatly throughout the world, according to the stable influences of legal requirements, religious customs and social traditions as well as to the unstable influence of economic conditions. In Western countries, at least, single women tend to be localized in towns; on the other hand, bachelors, especially old ones, tend to favour rural areas.

Marriage

Marriage is a legal fact, not a biological one like birth and death, and as its legality may be established by civil, religious or other means, marriage statistics of different countries are not easily comparable.

There are three forms of marriage:

(a) *Monogamy*, the marriage of one man to one woman;
(b) *Polygyny*, the marriage of one man to two or more women;
(c) *Polyandry*, the marriage of one woman to two or more men.

Polygyny and polyandry are two separate forms of *polygamy*, compound marriage. These forms of marriage may have profound influence upon fertility and population growth. Needless to say, however, demographic data of this sort are scanty.

Monogamy is the most wide-spread form of marriage. Nevertheless, the absolute monogamy enforced in the Western World today is fairly recent, for polygyny was legally accepted by Church and State as late as the middle of the seventeenth century.

There are few primitive tribes in which polygyny is impossible. Malinowski regarded it as multiple monogamy for which there is usually an economic or political motive. Normal sex-ratios reduce the frequency of polygyny within any particular community. In Africa, polygyny was often facilitated by abnormal sex-ratios caused by the slave-trade or, as in the case of the Baganda of Uganda, almost a deliberately high rate of male mortality. Polygyny is therefore often the prerogative of chiefs and rulers, who thus increase their prestige, labour force and followers. Some rulers have been prodigiously prolific: Sultan Moulay Ismail of Morocco (1672–1727) is supposed to have had 549 wives and was survived by 867 children. However, much anthropological evidence from Africa suggests that polygamous wives have fewer children than do monogamous wives, and that polygyny may be an important cause of the slightly lower fertility experienced in Negro Africa than might be expected.

Polyandry, a rare form of marriage, is often associated with female infanticide, and may be fraternal or non-fraternal; in the former case two or more brothers are married to one wife, as among the Todas of southern India, and in the latter case two or more unrelated men are married to one wife.

The number of marriages varies from year to year according to the number of people who reach marriageable age — a reflection of previous fertility and mortality — as well as to a host of other factors such as the state of the harvest, the level of prices, the period of military service, the rate of income tax and the political atmosphere. The number of marriages in any one year is also influenced by the number in the preceding year, so it is wise never to consider that number in isolation but to consider the number of marriages in a generation.

Marriage rates are useful, however, as measures of fluctuation in the frequency of marriage. The two most frequent methods used are:

(1) $(M/P) \times 1000$ or 10,000, where M equals the number of marriages during the year, and P the total population at the mid-point of the year;

(2) $(2M/P) \times 1000$ or 10,000, i.e. the proportion of persons married during the year.

Both are *crude marriage rates*, because they are not related to the number of marriageable persons.

Perhaps surprisingly, it is difficult to detect a major world pattern of age at marriage. Although in primitive communities marriage takes place much earlier in life than it does in advanced communities, the Woytinskys found that "contrary to widespread opinion, there is no universal tendency towards later marriages in economically developed and urbanized countries". In fact, there is a marked trend towards earlier marriage in western Europe as well as in many countries of European tradition, due not only to changed economic conditions but also to a change in attitude towards marriage. At the same time, the proportion married is higher than before.

In Britain, this trend is characteristic not merely of the post-war period, but of the whole twentieth century, and it is more obvious in towns than in rural areas. In general, however, the proportion of married women, and to a lesser extent married men, is lower in towns (especially large towns) than in rural areas. This situation is also true for some towns of Tropical Africa, owing to the breakdown of marriage systems and the desire of women for economic independence.

Widowhood

Widows are more common than widowers, because men marry later, have a higher mortality and re-marry more often than women. In Great Britain widows are about four times as numerous as widowers, and the widowed population numbers over 3·5 millions, about 7 per cent of the total. Nearly two-thirds are over 65, and despite State assistance they constitute a special problem, which however is not unique to this country. Widows' weeds are all too much in evidence in France. In modern society the problem is aggravated by the looseness of family ties, especially in towns where widows, in particular, are most frequent. In Britain the proportion of widows is highest in spas and resorts which specialize in retirement, though the problem is often more acute in poorer-class areas. But our problems seem small in comparison with India, where in 1961 there were 23 million widows enumerated and over 8 million widowers.

Divorce

As the social and economic ties of the family may become weakened in modern societies, affection, children and religion come to be the only remaining bonds, and so relaxation in divorce legislation inevitably leads to an increase in the number of divorces.

The divorce rates may be measured in three ways: (a) as the number of divorces per 1000 or 10,000 inhabitants, (b) as the ratio of the number of divorces to the number of married couples, or (c) as the ratio of the number of divorces to the average annual number of marriages in the preceding decade.

Once more international comparison is difficult because the causes of divorce and the legislation for divorce vary so greatly. In some Moslem countries divorce is a commonplace and is easily acquired, while in many Roman Catholic countries, like Spain, Italy, Ireland, Malta and many South American republics, the institution of divorce is ignored. The divorce rates of the U.S.A. and the U.S.S.R. are much greater than those prevailing in Europe, where Britain has a lower rate than most other countries. Nevertheless, in England and Wales divorce ends nearly one in ten of first marriages, the majority of which are childless, and ends more marriages than does death in age-groups under 50. Before the war the number of divorces never exceeded 8000, but following a revision of divorce legislation in 1937 there was a great growth in the number of divorces in the post-war years (1947: 60,254 divorces in England and Wales), a situation common to most countries engaged in the war. The divorce rate subsequently settled down to about one-half of that of 1947, but rose steadily throughout the 1960s. In general, it is higher in towns than in rural areas, owing to different social attitudes as well as economic conditions.

Most divorced persons soon re-marry, and often start new families. Re-marriage is an important aspect of fertility studies, especially for instance in Moslem countries.

4. FAMILIES AND HOUSEHOLDS

The two terms family and household require definition. *The family* is a social group based on marriage and united by ties of kinship, with a common culture and a common household. It is a small unit at the base of the social structure, but it is the most widespread of social groups. *The household*, on the other hand, is not necessarily a family, for it merely means a group of people living together. The number and size of families and households greatly influence the character of settlement, and that is of considerable geographical significance.

The Forms and Sizes of Families

The simplest form of family is the *nuclear, elementary, primary or conjugal family*, which comprises father, mother and children. For statistical purposes, a husband and wife without children also constitute a family, and often widowed and divorced persons as well; all other relatives are excluded. This is the definition generally used by demographers, except in fertility studies when only the children are considered.

The average family size is the average number of live (or total) births per marriage, and may be calculated for:

(a) married women of various age-groups;

(b) generations of married women of completed fertility, i.e. past the childbearing age;

(c) cohorts (a group of married women whose marriages occurred in the same year) of various durations;

(d) cohorts of completed fertility.

These indices take into account married women without children, and naturally show nothing of the frequency distribution of family size. Nevertheless, they are useful for geographic comparisons.

In many societies, however, the family includes a much wider group. These *extended families* may result from (a) polygamy, (b) the common residence of primary families, forming a *joint family*, or (c) the common residence and kinship of primary families, forming a *clan*. The last two types of extended family are linked either through paternal or maternal lines, and descent may be *patrilineal* or *matrilineal*. Moreover, amongst many preliterate peoples the husband may go to live with the family of his wife, in which case the residence is termed *matrilocal*; on the other hand, when the wife lives with her husband's family, it is termed *patrilocal*. These types of residence depend considerably on the mode of life and the occupations of the sexes, and thus on the environment.

In fact, we may distinguish two broad types of family, the maternal and the patriarchal. Maternal families — it is doubtful whether absolute matriarchy ever existed in primitive society — are widespread among primitive peoples, but rare in civilized communities. On the other hand, the compact functional unit of the patriarchal family has been characteristic of most civilizations, including Europe from the Middle Ages until the nineteenth century, and India, Japan, the Arab countries and many other parts of the world today. In China it has been submitted recently to radical alterations by the communist régime, which regards it as "feudal". The patriarchal family is an important economic unit found especially among rural communities and existing in many sizes, but in Europe it has foundered with industrialization, urbanization and family limitation, and has been replaced by the modern democratic family, which is smaller, less authoritarian, more romantic and with more freedom for the individual. Here the family is no longer a production unit; its economic functions have changed with the increased education of women and their greater economic independence. Moreover, the state, the church and social organizations are controlling and replacing the family in many ways, and so the social functions of the family are diminishing.

Similar trends may be observed with modified features in North America, Australasia and other countries where ageing populations are characteristic, although the date of commencement and the rate of decline of family size differ locally. Large families are disappearing and small families and childless couples are increasing. This is sometimes known as the "spread of the small family system", and is largely the result of family limitation. It is not a universal phenomenon, and family size varies according to occupation and social status, intelligence and education, religion and region. In Britain, as in some of the above-mentioned countries, the first decline in family size was among the professional and salaried classes in the later nineteenth and early twentieth centuries, and only after the First World War did the decline spread to all other classes. Thus the gap between the sizes of upper and working-class families is diminishing. Rising standards of living and more general education have certainly helped to reduce the class differential. In Sweden, family size conforms more or less directly with income-group; the highest income-groups have the largest families. This precedent may eventually prevail in many other countries.

In Britain, the fall in family size is most evident in commercial and residential towns, and less in industrial, mining and agricultural areas. One must not infer, however, that the urban environment always encourages small families. Although in industrialized countries the family compositions of urban and rural populations differ markedly, this contrast is not evident in many countries where towns have been little affected by industry.

The influence of religion is certainly not uniform, and is mostly modified by other social and economic factors. The average size of Roman Catholic families in Britain, for example, is larger than that of non-Catholics, and this may help to account for the large size of families in Merseyside. However, religion cannot explain the great contrast in family size between Ireland and Malta, two fervent Catholic countries.

The Classification of Households

The term household involves great difficulties of definition. Most countries distinguish between *private households* and *institutional households* (also known in Britain as non-private households). The latter generally include groups of persons living in schools, hospitals, hotels, military installations and other institutions. Private households pose the greater problem of definition. The United Nations have recommended that a *private household* should be considered as "persons who jointly occupy the whole or part of a housing unit, usually share the principal meals and have common provisions for basic living needs; a person living alone or occupying a separate room in a part of a housing unit, but who does not join with any of the other occupants of the housing unit to form part of a multi-person household, is considered to constitute a separate household". This definition of a private household is fairly widely accepted and is known as the housekeeping unit concept. However, it differs from the household–housing unit concept employed in countries like the U.S.A., Canada, New Zealand, Sweden, Iran and Czechoslovakia, where a lodger is included as a member of the host household. In Japan, lodgers are tabulated together with institutional households to form a group known as quasi-households.

Within households it is possible to identify families, who are persons related by blood, marriage or adoption, although in many cases the family and the household will be the same. For census purposes the primary unit is the *family nucleus*, which is the family in the narrow sense, namely a married couple with or without children, or a lone parent, married, widowed or divorced, if accompanied by one or more children. Obviously, private households may then be classified into

(a) *non-family households*, which may be one-person or multi-person (related or unrelated);

(b) *one-family households*: and

(c) *multi-family households*, which may be subdivided according to the number of family nuclei they contain and to whether they are related or not.

Families and households may be analysed in a wide variety of ways, but it is important to remember distinction between them, the former being essentially of biological significance and the latter an economic concept.

Patterns of Households

Study of areal variations in the number and size of households throws considerable light on patterns of social organization as well as demographic trends. We should note, however, that the average size of household — a common index — is usually slightly higher than the average size of private household, because of the greater size of institutional households.

In England and Wales we have witnessed a great increase in the numbers of households, owing to more marriages, earlier marriages and smaller families. They have risen from just below 8 millions in 1911 to 14,703,000 in 1961, and during these 50 years the average size fell from 4·54 persons to 3·13. By 1961, some 9,362,000 of all private households had no child under age 15, and 3,154,000 had only one child. Nearly one in seven contained only one person; this does not imply that all such persons are living entirely alone, but it is indicative of family fragmentation.

Lawton has examined (a) patterns of household size, (b) changes in numbers of households, and (c) ratios of households to dwellings in England and Wales, and has demonstrated the complex relationships between population distribution, households and dwellings. Average household size does not exhibit any clear regional pattern, though it ranges from 3·39 persons (1961) in the Merseyside conurbation to 2·93 in the West Yorkshire conurbation. The conurbations, along with remote rural areas in the north and west, also experienced a decrease in the number of households between 1951 and 1961, associated with an absolute loss of population. "The most notable increases in the number of households were in areas peripheral to the large towns and in regions of expanding industry." Such areas also recorded substantial increases in the number of dwellings during the 'fifties, although the patterns were not precisely similar. By determining the ratio of households to dwellings, Lawton was able to show that the main regions with a deficiency of dwellings were Greater London, the West Midlands, South Wales, Merseyside, Manchester and parts of north-east England. The problem in London was particularly aggravated by the high proportion (22·2 per cent) of one-person households. Such households are most characteristic of urban society, which has fewer roots, fewer family bonds and is more mobile than rural society.

5. ECONOMIC COMPOSITION

In the remainder of this chapter we shall examine aspects of population composition which are not strictly demographic, aspects which influence demographic trends only indirectly. In this section, however, we limit our attentions to the active population, its industrial and occupational structure, industrial status and socio-economic composition.

Active Population

The economically active population or labour force, which is distinct from the labour supply as it takes into account neither efficiency nor working hours, is variously defined as:

(a) *The population of working age:* broadly speaking, the adult population.

(b) *The working population:* including men and women who are normally employed, but who may be temporarily unemployed.

(c) *The employed population:* that actually engaged in productive employment at a given time. With the unemployed it forms the working population.

For international statistical purposes the second definition, that of the working population, is preferred by the United Nations, which includes in the definition the following types of persons:

"(a) Unpaid family workers, as well as employers, employees, and own-account workers;

(b) civilians as well as members of the armed forces;

(c) employed and unemployed persons, including those seeking work for the first time;

(d) persons engaged even part-time in economic activities; and

(e) domestic servants".

The inactive population therefore incorporates not only children below working age and retired persons, but also students, housewives, inmates of institutions and people living from royalties, rents, dividends, pensions, etc.

The activity rate of a population is the proportion which is economically active, and may be expressed age-specifically. Comparisons of activity rates of different countries can be accepted only with reservations because of varied definitions and age limits used. Non-comparability of data is particularly applicable to the economic activity of women, and therefore activity rates are generally given for males only. There are also great national variations in the economic activity of youths and aged persons; there is no uniformity in the length of active life, and although the active population is sometimes equated with the 15–64 age-group we must not forget the arbitrariness of these age limits.

The size of the active population depends on demographic, social and economic factors. There is no doubt, of course, that it is fairly closely related to the size of the total population, but the demographic régime and age-structure are also important determinants. In young rapidly growing populations of underdeveloped countries the active population tends to be small and there is "heavy youth dependency" because of the high proportion of children; but, as we see in the table below, boys and old men play a great role in the economic activity of such countries. At the other extreme, advanced ageing at the apex and the base creates a state of "heavy old-age dependency". Other things being equal, the activity rate is highest when there is only ageing at the base, an intermediate stage of "light dependency" which prevails at the moment in most highly developed countries, but not for long. In developed countries there is the counterbalancing effect of the limited economic activity of the young and the old, due to social and economic changes in recent decades.

TABLE 6.1. MALE ACTIVITY RATES BY AGE-GROUPS (PER 100 MALES) OBSERVED IN OR ABOUT 1950 IN THREE GROUPS OF COUNTRIES CLASSIFIED BY LEVEL OF ECONOMIC DEVELOPMENT

Countries	Age-groups								
	All ages	10–14	15–19	20–24	25–34	35–44	45–54	55–64	65 and over
Underdeveloped	58·5	30·8	81·8	93·1	96·2	97·2	96·2	90·7	78·5
Semi-developed	57·3	8·6	70·9	91·8	96·1	97·1	96·0	90·0	62·5
Developed	61·5	4·9	68·9	90·7	96·2	97·2	94·9	83·5	40·6

N.B.—The criterion for the above classification of countries is here taken as the percentage of males employed in agriculture: underdeveloped 60% or over, semi-developed 35–59%, and developed less than 35%.

(Source: U.N., Population Studies No. 26, p. 52).

The three evolutionary stages outlined above are helpful but not clear-cut; for instance, although ageing at the apex is the main cause of the present reduction in the activity rates of western Europe, post-war bulges have accentuated the process. Wars and migrations also play havoc with prognostications of future activity rates, which are based on trends in age-structure.

Numerous other factors also influence activity rates. Economic changes are obviously instrumental, and so is the urban–rural ratio. The activity rates of women, children and old people living in agricultural communities clearly differ from those in towns. On the whole they are higher in the country, but again it is dangerous to generalize. In western countries urbanization initially had little effect on the high activity rate of children, but it reduced that of women, because there were fewer opportunities of temporary employment in the towns than in the country. But in this century the decline in fertility and in family size, so marked in the towns, accompanied by the rise in the status of women has released a large number of women for employment, for which there are greater opportunities due to changes in the nature of the economy. Counteracting influences have been trends towards earlier marriages and increased popularity of marriage. The proportion of women at work in the United Kingdom is highest among young single women aged 16 to 25, and is generally higher for single than for married women of the same age. At the same time longer education and improvements in social conditions have diminished the activity of children in the towns.

The levels of income and employment also affect activity rates, but there are many conflicting assessments of their importance. On the other hand, it is easier perhaps to assess the influence of the state of health of the population on activity rates; it is certainly true that physical disability is higher in poverty-stricken, economically backward countries than in highly developed ones, and efficiency lower. However, such countries probably benefit from the fact that they have a young labour force contrasting with the ageing labour forces of developed countries, in which there are reductions in the proportion of active young adults and increases of older adults.

Unemployment

Unemployment occurs in a number of forms, and may be (a) persistent and general, (b) cyclical, (c) of short duration, (d) structural, i.e. within a particular industry or occupation, (e) technical, caused by improved production techniques, or (f) concealed, i.e. where workers' productive powers are not fully utilized.

The effects of population trends on unemployment in industrialized capitalist countries is a matter of some controversy, but in underdeveloped countries it is generally agreed, though not easily proven, that population increase provokes disguised unemployment, especially in agricultural communities. This last is more generally known as underemployment, when workers could be occupied more efficiently, for more hours or for more days, and occurs in many forms. Although a particularly severe problem of underdeveloped countries, it is not easily measured. Even in developed countries data on unemployment must be treated with some caution, for sometimes they do not include youngsters seeking their first job, and more commonly they do not include many married women seeking employment but not registered as unemployed. Consequently, unemployment rates may be marked understatements, and therefore may not be a satisfactory criterion of economic distress; other factors such as the female/male employment ratio, the proportion of old people and the volume of outward migration may be considered very relevant.

Whatever the causes of unemployment, it is obvious that it varies widely nationally and internationally. The pattern of unemployment in industrial areas is one of considerable interest to the geographer, for it is not only the result of unequal distribution of natural and human resources, but also of economic specialization, the immobility of labour and industry and numerous other factors. In general, as the local economy gets out of step with current trends of economic growth, the employment structure becomes anachronistic.

Industrial Composition

The industrial classification of the active population refers to branches of activity, and it is based on the type of establishment, product made or service rendered. The list is very long and the Standard Industrial Classification of 1958 lists thousands of industries, classified into orders and sub-orders, which conform in general with the International Standard Industrial Classification of all economic activities issued by the United Nations. Further complications are the diversity of establishments within any one industry, and the rapid birth and growth of industries. Hence, there is a tendency to group industries into a limited number of categories, so that overall trends can be determined. The United Nations Statistical Commission has adopted a nine-division classification which is sufficiently restricted to be of great value for international comparisons and trends:

1. Agriculture, forestry, hunting and fishing;
2. Mining and quarrying;
3. Manufacturing industries;
4. Construction;
5. Electricity, gas, water and sanitary services;
6. Commerce;
7. Transport, storage and communication;
8. Services;
9. Not classifiable elsewhere.

The proportions employed in these nine industry groups vary markedly from country to country and from region to region. Scrutiny of Table 6.2 will reveal that variations are greatest in agriculture, manufacturing, commerce and services.

TABLE 6.2. PERCENTAGE DISTRIBUTION OF ECONOMICALLY ACTIVE MALE POPULATION BY
INDUSTRY GROUPS IN SELECTED COUNTRIES

Countries		Industry groups								
		1	2	3	4	5	6	7	8	9
Nepal	(1952)	91·7	—	2·2	0·3	—	1·8	0·5	3·3	0·2
Sudan	(1956)	86·9	—	2·2	2·7	0·1	2·6	0·9	3·2	1·4
Indonesia	(1961)	69·5	0·3	4·6	2·2	0·2	6·0	2·7	8·2	6·3
Ghana	(1960)	59·6	2·7	8·1	5·1	0·8	5·7	4·0	7·4	6·6
Ceylon	(1953)	50·7	0·5	9·4	2·4	0·2	9·6	4·4	16·1	6·7
Ireland	(1961)	41·0	1·2	14·5	7·1	1·2	12·7	5·8	10·6	5·9
Hungary	(1960)	34·8	4·3	23·3	7·3	—	4·7	7·0	8·3	10·3
Japan	(1960)	26·0	1·8	24·1	9·1	0·8	16·9	7·2	14·1	—
New Zealand	(1961)	17·7	1·0	25·4	12·6	1·7	16·0	11·6	13·6	0·4
Australia	(1961)	13·3	1·7	28·0	11·5	2·8	17·0	10·3	13·6	1·8
Hong Kong	(1961)	6·6	0·9	37·6	10·8	1·9	12·9	9·2	18·7	1·4
England and Wales	(1965)	3·5	2·5	36·2	7·1	1·7	14·2	6·8	28·0	—

Owing to the difficulty in comparing data of industrial structure, it is customary, following the work of Colin Clark, to analyse it in three groups or sectors:

1. *Primary activities*, including agriculture, forestry, hunting and fishing.
2. *Secondary activities*, including mining, quarrying, manufacturing, production of electric power and gas and construction.
3. *Tertiary activities*, including commerce, transportation and communication, and services of all kinds.

As seen in Table 6.3, which includes data of the same twelve countries, the three sectors simplify the complexity of industrial composition in the same way that three age-groups simplify age-structure, except that the division is more difficult because of the numerous activities which overlap into two sectors.

TABLE 6.3. PERCENTAGE DISTRIBUTION OF ECONOMICALLY ACTIVE
MALE POPULATION BY INDUSTRIAL SECTORS IN SELECTED COUNTRIES

Countries		Primary	Secondary	Tertiary
Nepal	(1952)	91·7	2·5	5·8
Sudan	(1956)	86·9	5·0	8·1
Indonesia	(1961)	69·5	7·3	23·2
Ghana	(1960)	59·6	16·7	23·7
Ceylon	(1953)	50·7	12·5	36·8
Ireland	(1961)	41·0	24·0	35·0
Hungary	(1960)	34·8	34·9	30·3
Japan	(1960)	26·0	35·8	38·2
New Zealand	(1961)	17·7	40·7	41·6
Australia	(1961)	13·3	44·0	42·7
Hong Kong	(1961)	6·6	51·2	42·2
England and Wales	(1965)	3·5	47·5	49·0

Comparison of the three sectors in different countries does not give a true indication of economic evolution unless combined with other criteria such as *per capita* income, age-structure and the growth and distribution of population. Moreover, the concept has escaped neither criticism nor modifications. In particular, the division of the three categories has been variously interpreted; mining is sometimes included in the primary sector. Nevertheless, the concept does illustrate the great contrast between, on the one hand, the few highly developed industrial–commercial economies where often less than one-fifth of the active population are engaged in agriculture and where employment in tertiary services may exceed that in industry, and on the other, the many underdeveloped countries where more than two-thirds or even four-fifths are in primary activities, especially agriculture. Between these two extremes is a varied and widely scattered assortment of mixed agricultural–industrial economies, with greatly contrasted urban and rural economies. In these countries the proportions in agriculture range from 20 to 65 per cent. In most the tertiary sector exceeds the secondary; in a few like the U.S.S.R., Hungary and Bolivia the reverse is true. Once again we are faced with the problem of establishing categories within a complete series, with no wholly satisfactory solution.

The pre-industrial era and the underdeveloped countries today are sometimes spoken of as "primary civilization", in which about 80 per cent of the active population are engaged in primary activities, especially agriculture, 5 per cent in secondary and 15 per cent in tertiary. Unfortunately, the growing proportion in the tertiary sector is often a sign of demographic pressure, with large numbers in this sector employed in domestic service, petty trading and other lesser functions. "Secondary civilization" is characterized by industrialization, rural depopulation and urbanization, by the growth of the secondary and tertiary sectors at the expense of the primary. This phase is typical of Britain in the nineteenth and early twentieth centuries, but rapid technical progress, saturation and the decline in the marginal utility of secondary products meant the transfer of an increasing proportion of demand towards tertiary services, whose marginal utility declines much more slowly. The proportion of the active population employed in secondary activities then stops increasing — in some cases even the absolute number declines — and there is a migration of labour from the primary and secondary sectors to the tertiary. Colin Clark demonstrated that high real income is always associated with a high proportion employed in tertiary activities, as in countries like the United States, the United Kingdom, Australia, Canada and New Zealand, where the tertiary sector represents over two-fifths of the total active population; but apparently we need not fear saturation. Some authors prophesy that indefinite technical progress will not automatically mean indefinite economic progress, and they believe that the economy will eventually become stationary with the vast majority of the active population employed in tertiary activities.

We may also analyse industrial composition according to such differentials as age, sex, marital status and ethnic composition. In Britain, for example, we find a much older population in mining than in defence; a female majority in the textile and clothing industries, the distributive trades and some services; the increased employment of married women in industry; and the localization of West Indians in certain industries. Another differential is the ratio of state to private employment; it may surprise some that over one-quarter of the total employed population in Great Britain is in the public sector (in central or local government or other public undertakings).

Towns lend themselves to functional classification based on the primary, secondary and tertiary sectors. Towns with an important primary sector include mining centres (if mining is included in the primary sector), Soviet "agrovilles" and many agricultural centres in developing countries. The secondary sector is dominant in a variety of industrial towns, from those with highly specialized activities, such as textile and engineering towns, to those with a wide range of manufactures. A dominant tertiary sector is characteristic of historic cities unaffected by industrialization, administrative and religious centres, military and market towns, inland and seaside resorts. In capitals of developing countries the tertiary sector is often predominant owing to the concentration of administrative services, army, police, banking and commercial services as well as the hordes of small shopkeepers, porters, taxi-drivers, labourers, etc. In contrast, many of the great capitals of Europe have a more favourable balance between the secondary and tertiary sectors. The same is true for great cities like New York, Sydney, Johannesburg and Rio de Janeiro, but not for Washington, Canberra, Pretoria and Brasilia.

Of special interest to geographers is the distribution of the industrial population, and changes in distribution due to population movements and labour mobility. One inherent difficulty in distributional studies is the divergence between place of work and place of enumeration, a divergence which has increased in recent decades with the evolution in motor transport, although comparison of workplace and residence enables measurement of the difference between day and night populations, especially of urban centres, as well as the main lines of journey to work across administrative boundaries. So geographers should be aware of the considerable limitations of census data for the study of location of industry. However, study of industrial composition does enable comparison of the functional roles and the degree of specialization of towns and industrial regions. We may examine the rise and fall of industries, industrial towns and industrial regions, and the general tendencies within a country, for once a country has passed the primary stage its industrial composition is in a state of perpetual flux, a state also engendered by the fact that men are more tied by their occupation than by the industry in which they are employed.

Occupational Composition

The occupation of an individual refers to his trade, profession or type of work, and thus an occupation may be followed in different industries. But occupation is often confused with industry, for the distinction is not always clear. The problem of classification is probably even more acute than in the case of industry; the 1951 Census of England and Wales distinguished over 40,000 occupations in 27 orders and 61 sub-orders, but for the 1961 census the classification was completely revised, making intercensal comparisons difficult. In many ways occupational classification reveals more about the population than a classification according to industry, for the occupation of an individual is probably more important to him than the industry in which he works, but statements of occupation are very prone to errors.

The problems in the geographical analysis of occupational data are similar to those in the study of industrial data: the wide range of categories, and the distinction between place of work and place of enumeration. Wilkinson has emphasized the care necessary if occupational tables are to be used in the analysis of location of industry.

International comparisons of occupational data are only feasible with a simpler classification, so the U.N. *Demographic Yearbook*, 1964 uses ten groups, as in the International Standard Classification of Occupations, with an eleventh group for members of the armed forces:

1. Professional, technical and related workers;
2. Managerial, executive and administrative workers;
3. Clerical workers;
4. Sales workers;
5. Farmers, fishermen, hunters, lumbermen and related workers;
6. Workers in mine, quarry and related occupations;
7. Workers in transport and communication;
8. Craftsmen, production process workers and labourers not elsewhere classified;
9. Service, sport and recreation workers;
10. Workers not classifiable by occupation;
11. Members of the armed forces.

Industrial Status and Social Structure

By industrial status we mean the condition of the individual in his occupation. Classifications are often simple, and usually the following five categories are adopted: employers, workers on own account, salaried employees, wage earners and unpaid family workers, though in some countries there is an additional category — members of producers' co-operatives. International comparability of industrial status is low due to varying categories and connotations. Moreover, because in Great Britain and several other countries there has been little change in industrial status over the years, the subject is often ignored by geographers — though classification of industrial status according to industry, occupation and region gives an illuminating insight into the social structure. It helps to explain some of the social contrasts between a mining village and an agricultural village, between an industrial town and a market town, between a naval port and a fishing port.

Social structure brings in a number of factors, like living standards, classes and social dependence, which are not easily analysed statistically. Nevertheless, societies can be classified in broad terms according to their social structure, as Derruau has shown in the following categories:

(a) Primitive rural society with a tribal structure, as in Negro Africa.
(b) Rural society with contrasting classes of landlords and peasants, as in Iran or southern Iraq.
(c) Traditional western rural societies with a high proportion of rural non-farm people, exemplified in Western Germany.
(d) Rural societies with numerous agricultural labourers, as found in Languedoc.
(e) Colonial societies with peoples of contrasting traditions, techniques and living standards, found in the northern and southern parts of Africa.
(f) Societies with small rural populations at high living standards, and large numbers employed in trade and commerce, as in Australia.
(g) Industrial societies with marked urbanization and marked segregation of classes.
(h) Communist societies with little differentiation in living standards, like Yugoslavia and China.
(i) Communist societies with marked differentiations in living standards, like the U.S.S.R.

The rates of evolution of these various societies differ considerably, bringing increasing contrasts in social structures.

Socio-economic Groups

In order to understand the relationships between economic factors and demographic trends, there has been analysis of "social class" and "socio-economic groups". The classification of social class is usually based on the unit groups of the classification of occupations, and in Britain the following five are used:

I. Professional
II. Intermediate
III. Skilled
IV. Partly skilled
V. Unskilled

with classes II, III and IV being divided into manual, non-manual and agricultural sub-groups. However, this classification is rather crude, arbitrary and unwieldy.

A more satisfactory and objective classification is that of socio-economic groups which are based on cross-tabulation of data on industry, occupation and industrial status. In the 1961 census of Great Britain 16 groups were derived:

1. Employers and managers in central and local government, industry, commerce, etc. — large establishments
2. Ditto — small establishments
3. Professional workers — self-employed
4. Ditto — employees
5. Intermediate non-manual workers
6. Junior non-manual workers
7. Personal service workers
8. Foremen and supervisors — manual
9. Skilled manual workers
10. Semi-skilled manual workers
11. Unskilled manual workers
12. Own account workers (other than professional)
13. Farmers — employers and managers
14. Farmers — own account
15. Agricultural workers
16. Members of armed forces.

Hall and Smith have combined these groups into three classes and have classified each local authority in England and Wales into one of six categories, depending on the socio-economic class composition of the male population. Their map of socio-economic categories for the 1961 census illustrates striking contrasts between different parts of the country, especially between north and south, as well as between town and country and within urban areas.

6. NATIONALITY

Nation and Nationality

Nation and nationality are difficult concepts, and definitions have been varied and confusing. The reason for this confusion is that the terms may include racial, linguistic, cultural, psychological or administrative considerations, or combinations of these. Geographers normally restrict the term "nation" to a group of people who are conscious of their own nationality, people with common sentiment, traditions and territory who wish to maintain their cultural unity free from political domination. A common language is often a feature of nationality, and a common religion may help, but homogenous racial stock is rare, and long historical tradition not indispensable. Indeed, none of these qualities is vital, save the sentiment of nationality and the desire for common government, peculiar or exclusive to the nation.

Nation and state are concepts not easily distinguished, because nations evolve within states, sometimes coincide with them (nation-states), and sometimes overlap them. Nation-states are much rarer than multi-national states; in Europe we have few examples of the former, save in the north-west, and often the complexity of nationalities has been a cause of strife. On the other hand, some of the countries where Europeans have settled have moulded themselves into nation-states despite the diverse origins of immigrants, because the latter have soon acquired a new allegiance. The U.S.S.R. has a policy to preserve its multi-national structure; there are about 108 nationalities, but figures vary from time to time and naturally the number will decline along with increased economic development, urbanization, communist impregnation and use of the Russian language. Nationality depends on sentiments which can easily be swayed by propaganda. At times nationality rouses profound passions, but passions are ephemeral, and nationality impermanent. It may have no deep roots, and may die when its purpose is achieved. Nevertheless, some national minorities preserve remarkable unity despite strong pressure, perhaps because they are minorities. Nation and nationality are therefore intangible terms, the criteria for which may vary widely. In one country race may be considered the best basis for definition, in another language, in a third culture.

Legal Nationality

Nationality in the sense discussed defies statistical analysis. Consequently, demographers prefer to limit the term nationality to its legal sense — that is, to *country of citizenship* (not merely citizenship). The study of nationalities therefore becomes the study of foreigners within sovereign states. We must, however, distinguish between foreigners and foreign-born, for the latter may include nationals of the country of residence. There are, in fact, two distinct types of data according to (a) country of citizenship and (b) country of birth. Although at first sight data of this sort might seem very useful for international comparisons, there are numerous difficulties. First, *de jure* and *de facto* censuses may differ considerably; the *de facto* census may include many foreigners in transit or on holiday who are excluded from a *de jure* count.

Secondly, the conditions of acquisition of nationality vary greatly; in some countries only recent immigrants are considered as foreigners, in others all persons of foreign origin are classed as foreign nationals even when they are born in the country of residence. The category "aliens" submitted in statistical returns is therefore as diverse as that of "nationals". Ease of acquisition of nationality is often a feature of underpopulated countries or those with slow demographic growth. France, for example, welcomes foreigners far more than does the United Kingdom, which issued less than 100,000 certificates of nationality in the first half of this century.

A third difficulty is that nationals of dependent territories and colonies have the citizenship of the controlling power. Thus, citizens of Portuguese territories overseas are citizens of Portugal, and only citizens of countries outside the Commonwealth are considered aliens in British-controlled territories. Yet citizens of the United Kingdom and Colonies born outside of the United Kingdom are not permitted free access into it.

Fourthly, declarations of nationality are often vague; Britons abroad, for example, are prone to declaring themselves English, Scots, Welsh or Irish. There is also frequent indiscriminate use of the terms "native" and "national". "Native" usually refers to birth within the state, but some countries, like the United States, interpret the term as including those of their citizens born at sea or in foreign countries. Therefore, international data of native-born and foreign-born people, the sum of which forms the total population, may not be easily comparable. Data of this type are more usefully classified on an exact place-of-birth basis, because they indicate sources of migrations. Used with country of citizenship data, they throw light on the naturalization of foreign-born people.

"Stateless" persons constitute a further problem; sometimes they are referred to as stateless, and sometimes according to their previous country of citizenship. Moreover, some people have acquired dual nationality, as, for example, those of Israeli and American nationalities. Finally, designation of place-of-birth or country of citizenship is sometimes complicated by boundary changes, as in Central and Eastern Europe. So it will be realized that while it is fairly easy to study foreigners within any particular country, it is more difficult to compare the data with those of another country.

The Distribution of Foreigners

There are tens of millions of people in the world who are classed as foreigners. They are most common in the countries of recent immigration, in the Americas and Australasia, but their numbers are often declining through rapid assimilation; the percentage of foreign-born in the United States dropped from 48 in 1910 to 5·4 in 1960. In South-East Asia, migrant Chinese are still numerous, and the partition of the Indian sub-continent has added further foreigners. In 1951, soon after partition, there were 678,102 Pakistanis in India and 127,831 Indians in Pakistan, although nearly $8\frac{1}{4}$ millions of the population of India were born in Pakistan and over $7\frac{1}{2}$ millions of the population of Pakistan were born in India. On the other hand, foreigners constitute only small minorities of these populous countries of Asia. Independence in Africa is posing great problems of nationality, especially as political boundaries inherited from European rule pay scant respect to tribal distribution. The division of the Somali nation by the boundaries of Ethiopia, Kenya, the Somali Republic and Djibouti is one example of the complexities of African nationalities.

In Europe immense reshuffles and hordes of refugees complicated the pattern of nationalities. West Germany has probably more foreigners than France, but France has exerted a more consistent attraction, not only on peripheral peoples — Belgians, Swiss, Italians and Spaniards — but also on Poles, who are second in number to Italians. Foreigners are found especially in the industrial regions of the north, in the frontier margins of the south and in Paris. Switzerland and Luxembourg, both surrounded by land, have a high proportion of foreigners but lower absolute numbers. The highest proportion of foreigners in a European state is found in the tourist resort of Monaco: 18,557 (85·2 per cent) of the total 21,783 people in 1962. (This is not a record; in 1950, 97·8 per cent of the 187,772 people in Macau were aliens.) The industrialized countries of western Europe are still a magnet, and Britain and Belgium have similar numbers of aliens. In 1960 there were 405,889 registered in the United Kingdom; by country of citizenship Poland headed the list (99,477), followed by the increasing numbers of Italians (68,145), Germans (42,305) and Americans (30,938). Several dozen other nationalities are represented, but this diversity is not unusual. Nor is the preponderance of males, and the congregation and segregation of foreigners within the capital, other large cities and ports. There foreigners usually find it easier and more profitable to establish themselves than within rural communities, where there are few opportunities for the unskilled or those with special skills, and where they might find themselves friendless. Except in captured countries, those desiring foreigners or in frontier zones, rural areas are virtually closed to the alien.

Wilkinson has examined the problem of mapping nationalities with respect to Macedonia, and has shown how social and political prejudice affects the viewpoint of the cartographer as well as the accuracy of the data.

7. LANGUAGE

Types of Data

Language is universal to mankind, but it is also one of the most significant differentials. The term itself is ambiguous, and much confusion also arises over the definition of the terms "dialect" and "accent". The lack of a uniform classification of languages has impeded the comparison of linguistic data of different countries. This problem is made more acute by the occurrence of three types of data:

(a) mother tongue, namely the language spoken by the individual in his home or in his early childhood;

(b) language currently or usually spoken in the home;

(c) the individual's knowledge of a specified language or languages.

The first type of data is that favoured by the United Nations, and it is the best for comparative purposes. The second and third types of data introduce difficulties of degree, but they do facilitate studies of linguistic assimilation of immigrants and linguistic diversity. Some of the difficulties may be envisaged when one considers the differences between those who speak only Welsh, those who speak both Welsh and English regularly and those who speak Welsh poorly and rarely.

Language Families

The languages of the world are extremely diverse; today they number about 2800, and often contain numerous dialects. Many languages belong to the same *stock* or *family*, they have common descent; the Indo-European, Semitic, Dravidian and Malayo-Polynesian families are well-known examples. Some language families are spoken by hundreds of millions of people, but others by only a few thousand. In the New World there are more than 1000 different languages belonging to over 125 families. They contrast immensely, for example, with the Indo-European family, which is probably spoken by 1000 million people and has nine sub-groups:

1. *Germanic*, including English, German, Dutch, Flemish and the Scandinavian languages.
2. *Romance or Latin*, including French, Spanish, Portuguese, Galician, Catalan, Italian and Rumanian.

3. *Celtic*, including Gaelic, Erse, Welsh and Breton.
4. *Slavonic*, including Russian, Polish, Czech, Slovak, Slovene, Serbo-Croat and Bulgarian.
5. *Baltic*, including Lithuanian and Lettish.
6. *Greek*.
7. *Albanian*.
8. *Armenian*.
9. *Indo-Iranian*, including Persian, Kurdish and many modern languages of India.

The numerous divisions of this family of languages are symptomatic of the rapid evolution and diversification of language. Without concerning ourselves with the main periods of the English language, Old English (A.D. 900–1100), Middle English (1100–1550) and Modern English (1550 onwards), if we compare our own language with that of our grandfathers we realize the constant changes. Many of these changes are due to inventions, and many are due to changing modes of life. Languages are intimately related to the environment and to man's activities.

The Spread of Language

Isolation, geographical and social, originally fostered the separate formation of languages and undoubtedly many were related to distinct modes of life. Distance and natural barriers like the oceans, the mountains, the jungles and the deserts restricted the extension of these languages or diluted their purity. A classic example is the increasing transformation of Arabic away from its central source towards the peripheries of the Arab world. The barriers to language spread are not all natural; contrasting cultural traditions and infrequent commercial intercourse have proved just as effective. Indeed, trade has enabled some languages, like English, French, Spanish, Arabic and Chinese, to spread over many parts of the world, although in places trade languages have developed, such as Swahili in East Africa, Petit Nègre in former French West Africa, and Trade Chinook in North America. Missionaries and migrants, conquerors and colonists have also introduced their languages to varied regions, but migrants who do not migrate as a community are ready to adopt a new language. On the other hand, community migrations, especially nomadic migrations, have been most powerful forces in the expansion of such language families as the *Ural-Altaic*, which originated in the steppes of central Asia and now stretches as far away as northern Europe (Finnish), the *Semitic* family of North Africa and South-West Asia, the *Hamitic* family of North and East Africa and the *Malayo-Polynesian* family of the East Indian archipelago, Madagascar, New Zealand and the Philippines.

Languages and Nations

It has been said that languages are the chief determinants of nations, that they are a source of common traditions and sentiment, a source of cultural unity far more powerful than race, with which they may have no close affinity. The creation of political frontiers and of national or official languages, diffused by the press, radio, television, literature and schools, has affected the linguistic pattern of the world; linguistic uniformity has increased behind national frontiers, and the languages of important powers have become international. English, for example, has become a *lingua franca*, and Erse, Gaelic and Welsh, three Celtic forms of speech which once included the dead languages of the Isle of Man and Cornwall, are confined to the remote western fringes of the British Isles. Yet within other European states there is still surprising linguistic diversity, due to regionalism and long cultural traditions. In the Iberian peninsula, linguistic differences, which originated during the Moorish conquest and the Christian reconquest, have fostered separatism, and so also in Belgium where Flemish and French are the two main languages. However, in France, despite survivals of Breton, Basque, Spanish, Italian and German along the fringes, separatism is weaker. Moreover, in Switzerland national unity is not marred by the occurrence of four languages: German, French, Italian and Romanche.

Multilinguism naturally increases the difficulties of linguistic mapping, and prevents an ideal solution for linguistic minorities, but the problem of the latter is accentuated by their desire to preserve their mother tongue and resist cultural assimilation. Most European countries contain such minorities.

Many of the new nations of the world owe little or nothing to linguistic uniformity; frequently a common enemy, usually a colonial power, gave more stimulus to struggles for independence than possession of a common language, religion or culture. Such was the case in Asia and Africa where, however, language differences may not pose as many barriers as they have done in Europe. The *Demographic Yearbook* for 1956 lists 283 languages spoken in India in 1951, excluding 333 separate languages or dialects for which speakers numbered less than one thousand each. Nineteen Indian languages each had more than one million speakers, and 12 had over 10 millions; and although Hindustani is the national language, English is still the language of the intellectuals. Differences of language have contributed significantly to the political difficulties between East and West Pakistan. Language differences have caused political disorders in Ceylon, where Tamils and Sinhalese are bitter rivals, and also in Indonesia, where there are at least 30 main languages belonging to the Malayo-Polynesian, Melanesian and Papuan groups, and where Malay is the *lingua franca*. In the Soviet Union it is Russian that is the common medium, but there the policy has been to encourage traditional languages along with traditional interests. In Africa, there is great linguistic diversity even within small countries, but as in the Americas colonial languages, in particular English, French, Spanish and Portuguese, are the official languages for much of the continent south of the Sahara.

8. RELIGION

Inadequacy of Data

As for many other aspects of population composition, there have been few systematic studies of the geography of religion. This partly results from inadequacy of data, which are more difficult to obtain than for most other demographic traits. Zelinsky has noted that "among the multiple definitions of religion we must include: a mental complex . . .; a highly diversified body of customs . . .; a formal institution, i.e. church or denomination; and a group of persons sharing some degree of religious identity by virtue of tradition or common observance." Should we therefore consider only formal adherence? If not, how do we measure religious practice or belief? For these and other reasons no question about religion has been asked in a British census since 1851, and in many other countries religion is not included in census question- naires. Religious differences are a principal reason for the lack of a census in the Lebanon. Moreover, it is not surprising that most approaches to religious geography have been concerned not with the religious composition of populations, but rather with the influence of the environment and modes of life on the form of religion, and the retroaction of religion on the environment, and on human activities and settlement forms.

The Distribution of Religions

Although it does not match linguistic diversity, the diversity of religions is considerable. The four great world religions, Christianity, Islam, Hinduism and Buddhism, certainly incorporate a large proportion of mankind — in 1965 the respective adherents of these religions were estimated at 970 millions, 430 millions, 425 millions and 225 millions — and cover a large part of the globe, but they do not form homogeneous stable blocs, nor are they devoid of internal schisms.

It is true that Islam, Hinduism and Buddhism (often combined with Taoism, Shintoism and Confucianism) have more or less compact spheres, on which Christianity has failed to make any deep penetration despite its spread to most other parts of the world; but in certain localities the pattern of religions is so complex that cartographic distributions are extremely problematical. The Middle East is one such locality, and is particularly interesting as a source of religions (Zoroastrianism, Judaism, Christianity and Islam) as well as a scene of religious conflict and of sectarian divisions. Another is Kashmir, which is culturally divided between Islam, Hinduism and Buddhism. A third is south India and Ceylon, where Buddhists, Hindus, Christians and Moslems are all found in large numbers. It should be stressed that although the broad pattern of the main religions has appeared to remain fairly stable during this century, it is far from static; most religions are, on the one hand, gaining converts, but also losing agnostics, atheists, humanists, rationalists, etc. The southward spread of Islam in Africa is remarkably swift, particularly since decolonization and political independence.

Communism has gained immensely at the expense of religions, and the communist bloc now occupies about one-quarter of the total area of the world and more than one-third of its population. Not all of these people are without religious beliefs, but the number with religious experience must inevitably dwindle in the face of communist propaganda. Among other reasons, some of the success of communism in Asia has been due to the fact that religion often seemed allied with backwardness, class division, a patriarchal society and social and economic degradation of the masses. Communist success is also due to its alliance with nationalism, and its imposition of uniformity at a national level.

Divisions and Dynamism

Religious conflicts, so fierce in the past, are not over. The appalling mass migration which accompanied the partition of India, the bitter enmity of Arab and Jew, and the troubles in Ireland, Cyprus and Ceylon are sufficient reminders of the divisive force of religion. Moreover, nobody should forget that the Nazis massacred about 5,800,000 Jews.

All the main religions are subdivided: Christianity has several great churches, the Roman Catholic, Orthodox, Coptic and Protestant; Islam is primarily split between Sunni and Shi'a; Buddhism is similarly shattered. But sectarianism goes much further. Shi'a Moslems include Qarmatians, Ismailis, Alawi, Druses, Zaidis and many others. Some of these are refuge communities. In the Middle East we also find a number of Uniate churches which accept the supremacy of the Pope, yet have widely different practices: the Greek Catholic, Coptic Catholic, Syrian Catholic, Armenian Catholic, Chaldean Catholic and Maronite churches. In the United States we find hosts of Protestant sects, which are mostly national in distribution, but also have one or more regional concentrations. This has enabled Zelinsky to delineate religious regions. Such regions could also be established in Britain, where churches are numerous enough and often with strong regional affiliation.

Divisions within the main religions are a separatist force, help in the formation of distinct cultural nuclei, and may be a source of national weakness. Few countries are fortunate enough to possess religious uniformity: the Scandinavian countries are amongst the most homogeneously Protestant and the Iberian and Latin American countries the most homogeneously Catholic. In contrast, Catholic–Protestant splits are strong in Canada and the United States and significant in the United Kingdom, Australia and New Zealand.

It is important to stress the dynamism of religions, whose forms change frequently, adapting themselves to varying conditions. Unfortunately, limitations in data impede our attempts to determine trends. Nevertheless, it is obvious that the ramifications of Christianity, for example, are far smaller now than in medieval times, when the role of the church included government. Moreover, in contrast to the idealistic religions of modern societies, religions of primitive societies are largely magical, an attempt to influence the supernatural in order to secure good fortune.

The main problem in religious geography is paucity of data. It will be realized that any examination of religion which is purely qualitative lacks penetration, so only in few parts of the world are we able to link the religious composition of the population either with man's activities and habitat or with his distribution, migrations and growth. At present religious geography is ill developed.

9. ETHNIC COMPOSITION

Man is a single species, and all types of human beings can interbreed. Many physical types are recognizable by criteria such as skin colour, hair structure and colour, eye colour and form, nasal form, head form, body form and blood groups, and numerous racial classifications of varying complexity have been proposed based on one or more of these criteria with categories ranging from 3 to 400. Although the term "race" should have been reserved for groups of mankind with a particular biological or physical make-up, carried forward by inheritance, it has been commonly understood to be a community rather than a physical stock. Unfortunately, the term has either acquired linguistic and cultural connotations of political significance, such as in the case of the Nordic Germans, or it has been limited to skin colour, in particular the difference between Negroes and whites. In both cases "race" has been associated with myths of social superiority and with social segregation, economic contrasts and problems of racialism.

Accurate racial classifications of mankind are impossible because the distributions of human characteristics do not coincide, and because the earlier division of mankind into isolated small populations is gradually breaking down as a result of greater human mobility. Consequently racial convergence is exceeding racial divergence, and the differences are becoming blurred. The merging of gene pools from different populations is producing large populations which have more individual variations than earlier more localized populations. This blending of peoples has often produced hybrid vigour, but has made the task of census enumeration of racial groups extremely

difficult. For example, how much Negro blood do you need to have in order
to be considered a Negro?

In view of the difficulties of racial classification and enumeration, censuses
usually distinguish between ethnic groups, based often on a combination of
biological and cultural criteria, including nationality, language and religion.
In some countries they may be referred to as minorities, and in others as
nationalities, but they invariably demonstrate demographic, economic and
social contrasts as well as different if not discrete distributions. Moreover,
diversity of ethnic groups may cause considerable political problems.

Nearly all societies exhibit ethnic diversity, especially in their primate
and large cities, but certain parts of the world contain contrasting sizeable
ethnic groups intermingling or in juxtaposition. Such multi-racial or plural
societies are found especially in those regions affected by former European
expansion, as in Latin America, South-East Asia and southern Africa. Here
one finds four distinct types of ethnic group:

(a) the indigenous people, such as the Amerindians, Malayans and Bantu;
(b) the European colonists;
(c) the coloured peoples who were brought in as slaves or indentured
     labourers, or came as traders;
(d) the mixed peoples, such as mestizos, Anglo-Indians and Cape
     Coloureds.

The problems of plural societies tend to be greater where intermingling is
least, and so are generally less marked in Latin America than in South-East
Asia. They become most difficult where social segregation is enforced, as
in the case of South Africa.

At a more localized level, studies of ethnic diversity within cities like
Durban, Singapore and Chicago throw considerable light on the complex
structures of the cities and the problems of their evolution.

It is not considered relevant in this short volume to consider other aspects
of population composition for which census data are rare or minimal: intelligence, educational status, literacy and so on. Nevertheless, all have significant
effects upon population growth, migrations and distributions. It is evident
that throughout this chapter we have approached what Zelinsky calls the
"cut-off points" between population geography and neighbouring disciplines.
We have no space to range over the borders.

References

1. *Age-structure:*
   COULSON, M. R. C., The distribution of population age structures in Kansas City,
   Ann. Assoc. Amer. Geographers, **58**, 155 (1968).
   DEWDNEY, J. C., Age-structure maps of the British Isles, *Trans. Inst. Brit. Geogr.*,
   43 (1968).

FRANKLIN, S. H., The age structure of New Zealand's North Island communities, *Econ. Geog.*, **34**, 64 (1958).
ROCHEFORT, R., Pour une géographie sociale de la vieillesse, *Revue de Géogr. de Lyon*, **40**, 5 (1965).
SCOTT, P., The population structure of Australian cities, *Geog. J.*, **131**, 463 (1965).
U.N. Population Studies No. 26, *The Aging of Populations and its Economic and Social Implications*, 1956.

2. *Sex-composition:*
CLARKE, J. I., Rural and urban sex-ratios in England and Wales, *Tijdschrift voor Economische en Sociale Geografie*, **51**, 29 (1960).
FRANKLIN, S. H., The pattern of sex-ratios in New Zealand, *Econ. Geog.*, **32**, 162 (1956).
SAVILLE, J., *Rural Depopulation in England and Wales, 1851-1951*, 1957.

3. *Marital Status:*
SMITH, T. E. and BLACKER, J. G. C., *Population Characteristics of the Commonwealth Countries of Tropical Africa*, Univ. of London Inst. of Commonwealth Studies, Commonwealth Papers No. 9, 1963.

4. *Families and Households:*
CARR-SAUNDERS, A. M., CARADOG JONES, D. and MOSER, C. A., *A Survey of Social Conditions in England and Wales*, 1958.
LAWTON, R., Recent trends in population and housing in England and Wales, *Sociological Review*, **11**, 303 (1963).
MARSH, D. C., *The Changing Social Structure of England and Wales, 1871-1951*, 1958.

5. *Economic Composition:*
CLARK, C., *Conditions of Economic Progress*, 2nd ed., 1951.
DERRUAU, M., *Précis de géographie humaine*, 1961.
HALL, C. B. and SMITH, R. A., Socio-economic patterns of England and Wales, *Urban Studies*, **5**, 59 (1968).
SALT, J., Post-war unemployment in Britain: some basic considerations, *Trans. Inst. Brit. Geogr.*, **46**, 93 (1969).
U.N. Population Studies No. 9, *Application of International Standards to Census Data of the Economically Active Population*, 1951.
WILKINSON, H. R., The mapping of census returns of occupations and industries, *Geography*, **37**, 37 (1952).
WOYTINSKY, W. S. and E. S., *World Population and Production*, New York, 1953.

6. *Nationality:*
GOBLET, Y. M., *Political Geography and the World Map*, 1955.
DOUGLAS JACKSON, W. A., *Politics and Geographic Relationships*, Englewood Cliffs, New Jersey, 1964.
WILKINSON, H. R., *Maps and Politics*, Liverpool, 1951.

7. *Language:*
BOTTIGLIONI, G., Linguistic geography: its achievements, methods and orientations, *Word*, **10**, 375 (1954).
DEMANGEON, A., La géographie des langues, *Annales de Géographie*, **38**, 427 (1929).
WAGNER, P. L., Remarks on the geography of language, *Geog. Review*, **48**, 86 (1958).

8. *Religion:*
BRUSH, J. E., The distribution of religious communities in India, *Ann. Assoc. Amer. Geographers*, **39**, 81 (1949).
DEFFONTAINES, P., *Géographie et Religions*, 1948.
FICKELER, P., Grundfragen der Religionsgeographie, *Erdkunde*, **1**, 121 (1947).
FLEURE, H. J., The geographical distribution of the major religions, *Bull. Soc. Royale de Géographie d'Égypte*, **24**, 1 (1951).
IMBRIGHI, G., *Lineamenti di Geografia Religiosa*, Rome, 1961.

DE PLANHOL, X., *The World of Islam,* 1959.
SOPHER, D. E., *Geography of Religions,* Englewood Cliffs, 1967.
ZELINSKY, W., An approach to the religious geography of the United States, *Ann. Assoc. Amer. Geographers,* **51,** 139 (1961).

9. *Ethnic Composition:*
BROOKFIELD, H. C. and TATHAM, M. A., The distribution of racial groups in Durban, *Geog. Review,* **47,** 44 (1957).
CHANG, S. D., The distribution and occupations of overseas Chinese, *Geog. Review,* **58,** 89 (1968).
NEVILLE, W., Singapore: ethnic diversity and its implications, *Ann. Assoc. Amer. Geographers,* **56,** 236 (1966).
SABAGH, E., Some geographical characteristics of a plural society: apartheid in South Africa, *Geog. Review,* **58,** 1 (1968).
TROLL, C., Plural societies of developing countries; aspects of Social Geography, *Proc., 20th Congress International Geographical Union,* 1964, pp. 9–33.

CHAPTER VII

PATTERNS OF FERTILITY

WE MUST first define terms for there is undoubtedly confusion over meanings. Even the word *birth* has some ambiguity, owing to the distinction between live births and still births. *Fertility* is the occurrence of live births, and must not be confused with *fecundity*, by which we normally mean reproductive capacity or the ability to have children. The term *reproduction* is the degree of replacement of individuals by others of the same age in the following generation; it is sometimes confounded with the word *natality*.

Fluctuations in Fertility

Fertility is one of the main aspects of population study, not only because it usually exceeds mortality (the occurrence of deaths) and migrations and is therefore the main determinant of population growth and a principal influence upon population distribution, but also because it is more difficult to understand than mortality. While mortality is essentially individual, inevitable and involuntary, fertility is none of these things, and is far less constant and predictable. Fertility can be more controlled, and may be more influenced by many social, economic, political and psychological factors. Moreover, unlike death, which may occur at any age, women give birth to children only during a comparatively short period of their lives, and so a large number of births during one year will probably not be followed by a large number in the following year. Consequently, fertility is often subject to more short-term fluctuations than mortality.

Unfortunately, many apparent fluctuations in fertility result mainly from shortcomings in the data. Birth statistics are often wildly inaccurate and when correlated with rough population estimates lead to very crude guesses at fertility. National figures of fertility are too frequently accepted because they are in print. It is fortunate that demographers of the United Nations have tried to evaluate the completeness and accuracy of vital statistics, though this is more difficult for a time series.

Illegitimacy is one cause of inaccuracy. Although most births are legitimate, there are considerable areal variations in rates of illegitimacy, which often reflect attitudes towards marriage; for example, they are extremely high in the English-speaking Caribbean — more than two-thirds of Jamaican births occur out of wedlock — and very low in Ireland.

Indices of Fertility

The *crude birth rate* is the most common index of fertility, and is merely the ratio of the number of live births in a period of time, usually one year, to the total population, often at the mid-point of the year. The fraction is invariably multiplied by 1000 or 100.

This easily calculated and familiar rate is really of value to demonstrate gross additions to the population through births and can also give a rough idea of fertility trends in a particular country. However, it has clear limitations as a fertility index. It can give only a very general idea of similarities and differences between countries and regions, as it does not take into account age and sex composition, and does not accurately reveal differences in the frequency of births among reproductive age-groups. One can also envisage a situation in which the birth rate remains constant over a period while in fact there is either a steady increase in the numbers of births per family or an ageing of the population. Migrations also greatly influence birth rates, because of the preponderance among migrants of young adults of reproductive age. Consequently, crude birth rates cannot be easily compared, nor can they be used to evaluate future prospects.

To overcome the effect of regional or urban–rural variations in age composition within a country for the purpose of comparing birth rates, we can standardize the latter merely by calculating the birth rates which would have occurred if the age-composition of an area had been that of the country as a whole. The computation is simple but laborious, and proceeds by weighting the birth rate in each age-group with the numbers in the national age-composition. This *standardized birth rate* can then be turned into a fertility index by expressing it as a percentage of the national birth rate.

A useful index for ascertaining fertility in countries of inadequate vital registration is known as the *fertility ratio* or child/woman ratio. It is usually calculated as follows:

$$\frac{\text{Number of children under 5}}{\text{Number of women 15–44}} \times 100,$$

though other age ranges and a constant of 1000 are sometimes used. Its main advantage is that it is a standardized rate; its main disadvantages are that it cannot be calculated annually, but only for the five years preceding a census, and that the numerator is composed only of those children surviving, not of those who were actually born.

The *general fertility rate* also avoids some of the deficiencies of the crude birth rate by changing the denominator from total population to number of adults in the reproductive age-groups — usually only women aged 15–49. A more accurate fertility rate expresses the number of births per thousand *married* women in the reproductive age-group. Birth rates may also be expressed age specifically, i.e. specific for the age of the mother or father:

$$\frac{\text{Number of births to mothers (or fathers) aged } x}{\text{Number of women (or men) aged } x} \times 100$$

and this may be calculated for legitimate or illegitimate births or both. But obviously *age-specific birth rate* tables are not easy to compare. The sum of the female age-specific birth rates (multiplied by 5 if quinquennial age-groups are used) provides another rate, the *total fertility rate*, which gives approximately the average number of children per woman living until 50, and has the advantage of taking account of the female age-structure.

World Patterns of Fertility

Fertility varies greatly in time and space. Birth rates range from about 10 to 60 per thousand, and fertility rates from 40 to 250 per thousand (for women aged 10–49). The highest levels of fertility, with birth rates of 40 per thousand and over and fertility rates of 120 and over, are found in Latin America (excluding Argentina, Chile and some West Indian isles), Africa and in South-West and South-East Asia. Unfortunately, most of the countries with high fertility have inadequate data, and we must employ estimated birth rates. They are particularly high for some tropical African countries, but their reliability is low; nevertheless, in a major region of very high fertility there are considerable differences between countries, some arising from variations in adult and infant mortality which are both high. More significant in terms of world population increase are the high levels of fertility in the more populous continent of Asia. Indeed, probably well over two-thirds of the world's population, mostly in hot countries designated as underdeveloped or developing, experience birth rates of 40 per thousand and over. The contrast between developed and less-developed countries is more marked than in the case of mortality. At the other end of the scale, low fertility, with birth rates of less than 25 per thousand, is common to nearly all developed countries of Europe, North America and Oceania as well as the U.S.S.R.

The world pattern of fertility is therefore strongly bimodal, with the bulk of the world's population experiencing high fertility, so that fertility is one of the best socio-economic criteria for distinguishing between developed and underdeveloped countries. So far only a few underdeveloped countries, mostly small, have made a major transition from high to low fertility.

Fertility Trends

The fertility patterns described above result largely from four major fertility trends:

1. Persistent high fertility in numerous underdeveloped countries of Latin America, Africa and Asia.

2. Recent decline in fertility in Japan and some underdeveloped countries.
3. Long-term decline in fertility in many developed countries during the nineteenth and early twentieth centuries.
4. Fluctuating or stable low fertility in developed countries.

TABLE 7.1. BIRTH, DEATH AND INCREASE RATES FOR THE WORLD, CONTINENTS AND REGIONS, 1963

	Annual rate of increase (per 1000)	Birth rate (per 1000)	Death rate (per 1000)
WORLD TOTAL	1·9	33	14
AFRICA	2·5	45	21
Western	2·4	49	25
Eastern	2·5	42	17
Northern	2·7	46	19
Middle	2·0	44	24
Southern	2·4	40	16
NORTH AMERICA	1·2	19	9
LATIN AMERICA	2·9	40	11
Tropical South	3·1	43	12
Temperate South	1·8	26	8
Middle	3·4	45	11
Caribbean	2·3	37	14
EAST ASIA	1·5	32	17
Mainland	1·4	33	19
Japan	1·1	18	7
Other	2·6	38	12
SOUTH ASIA	2·6	41	15
Middle South	2·5	41	16
South-East	2·7	41	14
South-West	2·4	39	15
EUROPE	0·8	18	10
Western	0·9	18	11
Southern	1·1	20	9
Eastern	0·7	17	9
Northern	0·7	18	11
OCEANIA	2·0	25	10
Australia and New Zealand	1·9	21	9
Melanesia	2·3	42	19
Polynesia	2·9	38	9
U.S.S.R.	1·1	19	7

(Source: U.N. *Demographic Yearbook*, 1969)

Over vast areas of the world fertility remains high, a response partly perhaps to heavy mortality, but also a reflection of the extended family system and social customs of agrarian societies in which early marriage plays an important part. Far from experiencing a decline in fertility, some countries in South-

East Asia, Africa and Central America have actually witnessed increased fertility through reduced mortality. This has resulted especially from the prolongation of the lives of women in the reproductive age-group. These diverging levels of fertility and mortality have caused many in the West to question the desirability of "death control" without "birth control".

On the other hand, some countries have experienced a decline in fertility over the last few decades. Japan is the obvious example. Its birth rate fell from 34 per thousand in 1947 to 17 in 1962 (through a deliberate policy to reduce fertility), though a less precipitous decline had previously taken place

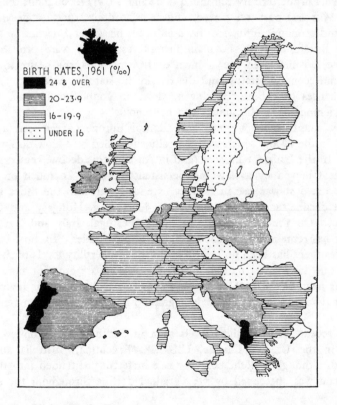

Fig. 18. Birth rates in Europe, 1961. North-West Europe no longer has markedly lower birth rates than the rest of the continent. The pattern is now more complex, especially in East Europe, where both very high and very low rates are found.

from 35 in 1920 to 26 in 1939. Lesser declines have also been recorded in Argentina, Uruguay, Chile, Cuba, Puerto Rico, Israel, Cyprus, Malaya, Hong Kong, Taiwan and Singapore as well as some Pacific islands like Fiji.

Much more prolonged falls in fertility were recorded in Western Europe and North America during the nineteenth and twentieth centuries. In France, Ireland and the United States they began in the early nineteenth century; in Scandinavian countries about mid-century; in the British Isles and Germany in the 1870s, and in Italy in the 1880s. The countries heavily involved in the First World War had a marked drop in fertility, followed by a post-war baby boom and renewed decline — until 1933 in Germany, 1935 in the U.S.A. and Canada, and the beginning or early part of the Second World War in the case of Britain and France. On the other hand, in Ireland and many countries of Southern Europe fertility continued to decline slowly throughout the Second World War and post-war period. There is no doubt that a wide variety of social and economic influences have induced this general decline in fertility, but in Britain at least the main factors responsible were probably later marriage, the increased use of birth control methods, the desire for higher social and economic status, and the rise in the status of women. The main consequences have been the slowing down in population increase and the preponderance of small families and households.

Many countries in Western and Central Europe experienced a rise of fertility in the 1940s, which was generally succeeded by a slow decline in the 1950s. In the United Kingdom (and in Austria) this decline ceased in 1955, and was followed by a slow but persistent increase. In much of Eastern Europe the post-war rise in fertility extended well into the fifties before a gradual decline, sometimes to very low levels (e.g. Hungary and Czecho-slovakia). On the other hand, in Spain, Portugal, Italy and Switzerland fertility has remained remarkably stable since the fifties. In most European countries there has been no return yet to the low fertility levels of the 1930s, and as they have lower mortality their populations are growing more rapidly than for many decades. Nowhere is this post-war demographic revival more evident than in France, where demographic stagnation was imminent in the 1930s.

The recent stable fertility levels seen in South-West Europe were also found in the U.S.A., Canada, U.S.S.R., Argentina, Australia and New Zealand, although a slight post-war rise in fertility extended into the early fifties and was succeeded by very gradual decline throughout the sixties.

Differential Fertility

The fertility of a community is affected by a wide range of direct and indirect influences, which act as differentials so that there tend to be groups within populations whose fertility departs from the national average. For example, there tend to be substantial differences between the fertility of urban and rural populations, Negroes and Whites, Catholics and Protestants, miners and office workers, rich and poor. Such differences determine regional patterns of fertility, which are of special interest to geographers.

Demographic influences of particular significance are age-structure, the age, duration and frequency of marriage and the average size of family. Indeed, these three are primary axes of fertility investigations. Comparison of birth rates and fertility rates shows the importance of age-structure; Japan's birth rate in 1962 was 17·0 per thousand and similar to that of Norway, which was 17·3, but really her fertility rate (51·0 per thousand) was much lower than that of Norway (63·7) because her age-composition was more youthful. Similarly, rural fertility is often very much higher than birth rates imply, because migration has reduced the numbers in the 20–40 age-groups. For this reason also, it is often useful to analyse marriage rates by age-group rather than in general, as they demonstrate more accurately the true significance of marriage on fertility. Under conditions of little fertility control, age at marriage may be the key parameter of total fertility, and in low-fertility nations marriage generally occurs five years later than in high-fertility nations. We should also recall that polygamy has some influence on fertility, and evidence from Africa shows that polygamy probably reduces fertility (see Chapter VI).

Among the direct influences upon fertility family limitation is of paramount importance. By this term we include birth control, sterilization, abortion and abstention. Birth control has been mainly responsible for the major reduction in fertility in the developed countries, but the effects of abortion have been strikingly emphasized in Japan since its legalization in 1948; it has been the main cause of the decline of Japanese fertility. To many demographers family limitation is the only rapid solution to the "population explosion" so apparent in Asia. Religious attitudes to birth control are often responsible for contrasting fertility levels of religious groups; they account, for example, for the higher fertility of Catholic French-Canadians over that of English-speaking Protestant Canadians.

In principle, however, most religions favour fertility, and some exalt large families. In contrast, some philosophies fear fertility, and among these Malthusianism and its modifications have had great effects on European fertility. Social customs in primitive societies are influential, such as age at marriage and prohibition of intercourse between husband and wife during the suckling of a child. In consequence, not all African tribes have uniformly high fertility; the Azande of the Congo are actually diminishing through low fertility. Ritual promiscuity in some instances spreads venereal diseases which lower fertility. But health in general is a differential.

In many parts of the world rural fertility exceeds urban fertility. This is so in much of Europe and has been noticed in many less-developed areas, like Zanzibar and the Congo. There the presence of wealthier urban classes, who are aware of birth control methods, may be a factor. Rapidly growing towns may have fairly high fertility because the immigrants are mainly young adults who may preserve their rural demographic habits. From evidence in India, however, it has been suggested that differences in rural and urban fertility ratios are probably caused by differences in infant mortality, which is much lower in cities. This may be the case elsewhere. Nevertheless, there is some truth in the generalizations that fertility is inversely related to the size of the urban area, and that national fertility is inversely related to the urban-rural fertility differential. Low urban fertility is influenced by unbalanced sex-ratios, high living standards and costs, social capillarity, social classes, income groups, occupational status, female employment, educational facilities and attainments and so on, but there are no simple relationships. These factors help to explain the varying levels of urban fertility, and why central Scotland, Wales and northern England have higher fertility than south-eastern England. Rural societies also have differing fertility levels. In the United States rural-farm populations are usually more fertile than the rural-nonfarm. In Europe, farm labourers are usually more fertile than small-holders, just as miners are more fertile than textile workers. Occupational, industrial and social structures are clear fertility differentials. They have also some influence on the fact that foreign-born groups are often more fertile than native-born populations.

Hawley has suggested that there are three phases in the relationship between socio-economic class and fertility. In the first phase the classes have similar fertility; in the second, which began in the industrial nineteenth century, there is an inverse relationship; in the third phase there is a direct correlation. Sweden was one of the first countries to achieve this third phase, wherein the wealthier people have the most children.

Economic conditions and technical advance are equally pertinent. Yet economic prosperity may favour fertility in a young population, while having little effect on a more aged population. There the effects of economic crises are usually more apparent. Young, sparsely populated countries in phases of expansion, like America and Australia in the nineteenth century, need man-power and experience high fertility. Subsequently, the rural areas which depend on monoculture and mechanization require less labour than more intensively farmed areas, and their populations are often less fertile. Likewise, areas of vineyards and market gardening frequently have higher birth rates than areas of cereal cultivation or livestock farming. George considers the rate of economic development to be a major factor in regional fertility, and points to the slow economic and demographic progress in the Midi of France in contrast with the more virile north. On the other hand, rates of economic progress are associated with reverse effects in Italy, where the developed north has lower demographic fertility than the backward south. In Spain, also, industrialization in the Basque and Barcelona regions has had different demographic reactions. In other words, there is no simple relationship between regional economic conditions and population fertility; each region merits close scrutiny.

Racial groups often demonstrate differential fertility, though few countries adequately classify births according to colour or race. In New Zealand, Maori fertility is much higher than that of Whites, and similarly the fertility of the indigenous populations of Rhodesia and Zambia is almost twice that of the Europeans. In Brazil in recent years, Whites have been reproducing more rapidly than Negroes, though this may be largely because of lower infant mortality. American Negroes, however, are more fertile than their White compatriots, although urban–rural residence may be a significant influence there. Indian women in East Africa are more fertile than European women living there — these examples of race differentials could be multiplied.

Although all aspects of differential fertility cannot be covered adequately here, mention must be made of political influences. We include not merely the political policy of a government, its engagement in wars and alliances, but also its programmes of regional economic development and its attitude to population growth. Government direction of industry to a depressed area may well encourage renewed fertility, and so may a change in approach to farming. Measures concerning birth control, abortion, sterilization, ante-natal and post-natal care, family allowances and marriage loans may well be instrumental in their effects on fertility. Population policies in Nazi Germany, Fascist Italy and wartime Japan greatly stimulated fertility; Malthusian measures in Scandinavia have been effective in maintaining low fertility. In general, population policies are most efficacious when they conform to the general policy of the country and to the prevailing psychology (see pp. 152–5).

Inadequate data are the main deterrent to differential fertility analysis, especially by geographers, who have shied off areal studies of fertility. And yet there is great scope in this field, which has close links with other aspects of society and economy, and many indirect relationships with the environment.

References

BERELSON, B. *et al.*, *Family Planning and Population Programs*, Chicago, 1966.

CHO, L. J., Estimated refined measures of fertility for all major countries of the world, *Demography*, **1**, 359 (1964).

Demography, Progress and problems of fertility control around the world. Special issue, vol. 5, no. 2 (1968).

GLASS, D. V. and GREBENIK, E., *The Trend and Pattern of Fertility in Great Britain: A Report of the Family Census of 1946*, 1954.

HEENAN, B., Rural–urban distribution of fertilities in South Island, New Zealand, *Ann. Assoc. Amer. Geographers*, **57**, 313 (1967).

KISER, C. V. and WHELPTON, P. K., Social and psychological factors affecting fertility, *Milbank Memorial Fund Quarterly*, **36**, 1325 (1958).

LORIMER, F., *et al.*, *Culture and Human Fertility*, UNESCO, 1954.

STYCOS, J. M., *Human Fertility in Latin America*, New York, 1968.

CHAPTER VIII

PATTERNS OF MORTALITY

Characteristics of Mortality

Mortality, the occurrence of death, contrasts with fertility by being more stable and predictable, and less prone to mysterious fluctuations. We are interested in mortality not only for its effects upon population change, but also for its effects upon population-composition, especially age-composition, since mortality and longevity are closely linked.

Death control is more acceptable than birth control. The decline of mortality now taking place in so many of the underdeveloped countries has been in great measure due to medical progress, which was initiated in few parts of the world but has been rapidly applied to large sections of humanity, even those living at low technical levels. The decline of mortality has consequently been more widespread than the decline of fertility, and it is the increasing longevity of most of the world's inhabitants which is particularly responsible for the much-feared "population explosion". Indeed, it is one of the most important features of the recent history of mankind. In view of the demographic significance of mortality and its manifold social and economic effects, geographers must be interested in its distributional patterns.

Fortunately, geographers have shown less indifference to mortality than to fertility. In particular, the geographical study of mortality has proved vital in medical geography, a rejuvenated branch of our subject, partly because of the inadequacy of morbidity data over most of the world. Medical geographers tend to depend on "causes of death" data rather than on "causes of illness", but even crude mortality data are adequate for only a half of mankind.

Fortunately, crude mortality data are often more continuous and reliable than fertility data, though there is generally a tendency for them to be below reality. In Britain, at least, registration by John Graunt of deaths during epidemics in London in the seventeenth century antedates comparable collection of fertility data. We are also lucky that deaths are recorded by place of usual residence rather than place of occurrence, so that undue prominence is not given to towns. Moreover, data are available for small administrative areas.

One of the main problems in mortality data has been the recording of infant mortality and its distinction from foetal death. Ordinary mortality data should refer only to persons born live, and should exclude stillbirths, or late foetal deaths. *Stillbirth ratios* (the numbers of stillbirths reported per thousand live births) are distinct calculations.

Indices of Mortality

The *crude death rate* is merely the number of deaths per thousand inhabitants and may be calculated for the population at the mid-point of the year or at the beginning of the year. The latter really expresses the probability that the population has of dying during the year. Just as with crude birth rates, crude death rates are only really satisfactory when used in the comparison of population groups with identical compositions. It is particularly dangerous to compare death rates of old and young populations. Young populations of backward countries which have experienced recent rapid decline in mortality may have much lower death rates than more aged populations of advanced countries. Crude death rates can be broken down to *mortality rates by cause*, which are the number of deaths in each cause group per 100,000 persons. *Age-specific death rates* and *standardized mortality rates* (S.M.R.s) are calculated in the same way as for fertility, and there is no need to reiterate their advantages and limitations.

Much of the analysis of mortality by age and sex has centred on *life tables*, which are based on observed mortality conditions. They were first compiled for actuarial purposes to analyse the effects of present mortality rates on future age and sex-composition, in order to calculate for each group the number of deaths, the number of survivors and the average expectation of life of the latter. Their accuracy is closely dependent upon the validity of the censuses and vital registration, and they are therefore only possible in advanced countries. There are five common coefficients.

1. The *life table mortality rate* is the basic function of the life table, and represents the probability of dying during a given age interval, usually one year. In graphic form, life table mortality rates give a J-shaped curve, with the lowest point about the age of 10. The curve is much the same for developed and underdeveloped nations, but mortality rates at all ages are lower in the former.

2. The *survival table* depicts the numbers of survivors at each age, starting with a round number like 100,000, the deductions being made from the above rates.

3. *Death tables* merely comprise the number of deaths at each age and for both sexes. The maximum number of deaths in any age-group is said to coincide with "normal life".

4. *Average expectation of life*, or average life, at each age is the number of

years of life expected to each of the survivors at any given age, assuming that the total number of years was equally shared between them. Average expectation of life at birth is less than after the first year, because of infant mortality, but thereafter the decline is usually steady. Expectation of life at birth is a better measure of mortality than the crude death rate, as it is not affected by the age-structure of the population.

5. *Probable or median life* is the duration necessary to reduce the population to one-half. The index is much less common than expectation of life.

Though of great demographic significance, life tables offer few possibilities for mapping. On the other hand, it is most illuminating to make comparisons between different communities within a country.

The significance of age in mortality is most evident with infants. *Infant mortality rates* are the number of deaths of infants under one year old per thousand live births, and are not quite the same thing as the age-specific death rates of children under one. In the computation of infant mortality rates no account is taken of the fact that some of the infants dying in a given year were born in the previous year. Infant mortality usually exceeds mortality during any other year, at least in underdeveloped nations, and reflects closely on the state of the health services. Its reduction is generally the first stage in mortality decline and in underdeveloped countries this may happen rapidly, so that infant mortality rates tend to vary independently of mortality rates at older ages. Unfortunately, published infant mortality rates are often woefully below reality, because of omissions of registration.

Three other rates are noteworthy here: (a) *perinatal mortality*, which occurs during "the period of prenatal existence after viability is reached, the duration of labour, and the early part of extra-uterine life"; (b) *neonatal mortality*, occurring during the first four weeks of life; and (c) *post-neonatal mortality*, occurring within the remainder of the first year. All are expressed per thousand live births, but only the last is of real significance to geographers, as internal or congenital causes are ordinarily responsible for the first two. Neonatal mortality varies little from one country to another, and scientific advance has done little to diminish it.

In many countries high infant mortality is succeeded by high mortality of children aged 1–4 years. In backward countries, half of the total deaths in any one year may be of children aged 0–4 years; in England and Wales, however, they account for about one-twenty-fifth. Mortality is usually lowest among the teen-agers.

All these forms of *reproductive wastage*, defined as the loss of life from the time of fertilization of the ovum until the fifth year of age, tend to adversely affect the numbers of males, particularly in developed countries, where there is little sex differentiation in the care of children.

One other rate, the *maternal mortality rate*, is equally indicative of the availability of health services. It represents the number of women dying from causes arising from deliveries and complications of pregnancy and childbirth per ten thousand live births, and differs substantially between developed and underdeveloped countries.

World Patterns of Mortality

The United Nations' estimate of the average death rate of the world's population about 1970 was 14 per thousand, two-fifths of the estimated birth rate. Countries with higher rates than this were mainly in southern Asia, Africa and parts of Latin America (with notable exceptions like Argentina, Chile, Venezuela and Uruguay). Many of the countries in these regions owe their high mortality to very high infant mortality (well over 100 per thousand, and sometimes over 300) and low expectation of life (under 50 years, and sometimes only 30), resulting from low standards of living, hygiene and medical care.

Despite high standards, infant mortality rates below 30 per thousand (Fig. 19) and 70 years, life expectancy, death rates in many West European countries, including Great Britain, are between 10 and 13 per thousand. Lower rates are impeded by ageing populations. However, in Scandinavia and The Netherlands, lower infant mortality, greater life expectancy and even higher standards of medical care permit death rates of less than 10 per thousand. Similar low rates in some countries of eastern and southern Europe result more from youthful age-structures than from superior medical conditions. In spite of these variations, the range of mortality in Europe is much less than that of fertility; in 1968 the highest death rate was 13·0 in Austria, and the lowest 7·6 in Poland.

Fairly youthful populations, high living standards and renewed fertility all help to account for the low mortality (death rates below 10 per thousand) in Australia, New Zealand, the United States, Canada and the U.S.S.R. These countries have been joined in recent years by Japan, Argentina, Uruguay and some other Latin American states as well as by a number of smaller countries whose mortality has achieved extremely low levels: Bermuda 6·6 per thousand, Puerto Rico 5·6, Iceland 7·0, Taiwan 5·0, Hong Kong 5·0 and Singapore 5·5. In many of these small countries, the great gap between fertility and mortality poses severe problems of natural increase.

Mortality Trends

World variations in mortality are smaller than variations in fertility, and in many parts of the world a levelling is discernible which is tending to invalidate

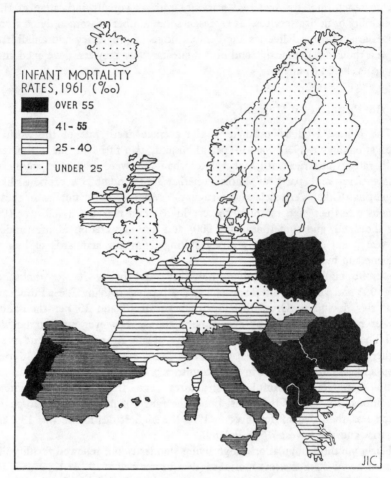

FIG. 19. Infant mortality rates in Europe, 1961. North-West contrasts with
South-East and South-West Europe.

former correlations between mortality levels and economic advancement.
There would appear to be more equality in the face of death, which will
eventually reduce the influence of mortality upon population growth, leaving
fertility as the main determinant.

In general, we may think of two phases of mortality decline. The first
occurred in the eighteenth, nineteenth and early twentieth centuries in the
advanced countries of Europe, North America and Australasia. It began in
the eighteenth century in Scandinavia, after 1820 in England and Wales, and
in the last quarter of the nineteenth century in most of the rest of western

Europe. Improved sanitation and housing, better food and water supplies, rising standards of living and working conditions, and later the growth of medical science all contributed to this decline in mortality, although the relative significance of the various factors has been the subject of much speculation. The rate of decline has diminished in this century, except in the U.S.S.R. and countries of south and east Europe, which used to lag behind, and still do in infant mortality (Fig. 19), but are now catching up. In most of the advanced countries, mortality decline has been arrested by the ageing of the population caused by low fertility, and the problem is no longer infant mortality but the diseases of the aged, like cancer and heart diseases. In some there has even been a tendency to increased mortality among older people — possibly owing to reduced mortality earlier in life. On the whole, future improvements in mortality among the advanced countries will probably be only minor and gradual.

In contrast, many of the underdeveloped countries enjoyed no appreciable decline in mortality until the last two decades, but then the fall, assisted by youthful age-structures, has sometimes been spectacular. Some countries, like Jamaica, Costa Rica and Puerto Rico, have benefited greatly from the introduction of medical knowledge and campaigns against infectious diseases, and have experienced considerable increases in life expectancy — often without comparable economic advance. But progress in mortality reduction has been unequal; it has been most striking where accompanied by rising standards of living, and therefore has been slower in India than in Ceylon, in Brazil than in Venezuela. Disparities in mortality levels are much greater in underdeveloped regions than in advanced regions, especially between different social classes, economic classes, racial groups and between urban and rural societies.

The 1970s and succeeding decades are likely to bring further reductions in mortality levels in many underdeveloped regions. By 1980 the majority of the world's inhabitants may have a life expectancy at birth of 65 years, but for this to happen there must be great changes in Asia and Africa, where malnutrition, poverty and illiteracy are severe barriers to mortality decline.

Differential Mortality

It is worth reiterating that age and sex-structures are key factors in mortality, and that the mortality of males is higher than that of females at almost every age in all but a few underdeveloped countries. Moreover, the gap is widening, and evidence seems to suggest that the causes are mainly biological. The same is probably true for the lower mortality of married persons than unmarried — in general, healthier people get married.

On the other hand, levelling of mortality of Negroes and Whites in the United States and of Maoris and Europeans in New Zealand seems to indicate that biological differences have not been the main cause of differential mortality between racial groups; social, economic and environmental conditions have been largely responsible. The massive reduction of mortality in Japan to a level comparable with western Europe and North America is also relevant. However, in South and East Africa, race differentials in mortality are still striking, the European and Indian communities having much lower death rates than the Africans (Table 8.1). This partly results from the geographical distribution of the non-African population, which is highly localized in towns, where hospitals and doctors (mostly Europeans and Asians) are found.

TABLE 8.1. CONTRASTS IN MORTALITY AND EXPECTATION OF LIFE IN SOUTH AFRICA

	Death rates per 1000 (1968)	Infant mortality rates, per 1000 (1968)	Life expectancy at birth (1959–61)	
			Males	Females
Whites	8·8	24·6	64·73	71·67
Asians	7·3	50·8	59·59	59·59
Coloureds	14·4	128·8	54·28	54·28

Urban–rural differentials in mortality have long been evident. At one time large cities in Britain were far less healthy than rural areas and suffered from higher mortality. John Graunt's *Natural and Political Observation Mentioned in the Following Index and Made Upon the Bills of Mortality*, which appeared in 1662, arose out of the fearful conditions in London at the time. Much later, Dr. John Snow was to demonstrate the value of the geographical approach to this problem by mapping the distribution of 500 deaths from cholera which occurred over 10 days in 1848 in the Soho district of London. Now the former urban–rural differential has been either greatly attenuated or removed by improvements in urban living conditions and the concentration of hospital and medical facilities in towns. For this reason, urban mortality is often much lower than rural mortality in underdeveloped countries. For example, the demographic sample survey of Guinea in 1954–5 revealed much higher survival rates for town children than for country children. But there can be no rules about the urban–rural differential. In advanced countries rural areas may have lower mortality because they are healthier, but there are often greater differences between towns than between town and country. Both Howe and Murray in their mapping of mortality in England and Wales have pointed to the higher mortality of old industrial towns of the north and west — in Lancashire, the West Riding, the North-East and

South Wales — and the much more favourable rates in towns of the south and east, like Canterbury, Oxford, Norwich, Bath and Reading. This applies not only to general mortality, but for most of the categories of causes of death. In fact, regional contrasts in rural rates are also apparent, especially between the lower rates of the more prosperous agricultural countries of Lowland Britain and the higher rates of the lower-quality farming areas of Highland Britain (Fig. 20). The contrast is even sharper for infant mortality. In France

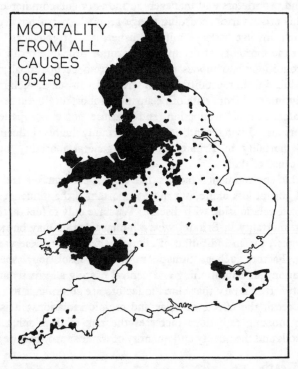

FIG. 20. Male mortality from all causes in England and Wales, 1954–8. Areas in black have above-average standardized mortality rates. Simplified from HOWE, G. M., *National Atlas of Disease Mortality*, 1963.

and Italy the north–south gradient is also clear, though in Italy the higher mortality in the north than in the south is associated with lower infant mortality and greater longevity. In advanced countries there are no simple relationships of regional mortality patterns, as are sometimes visible in less-developed countries. In East Africa, for example, we find the lowest death rates among the most advanced tribes, like the Buganda and Wachagga.

Socio-economic groups are obvious differentials. In general, the highest mortality is found among the poorest classes and the lowest among the wealthy, and this is especially true for infant mortality, but once again levelling is observable in advanced countries. Decennial studies of occupational mortality in England and Wales, initiated by William Farr in 1851, permit analysis of this feature. There is no longer a simple inverse relationship between social class and mortality. While it is true that mortality rates are still highest among unskilled workers (class V), skilled workers (class III) come next, followed by the professionals (class I), semi-skilled workers (class IV) and proprietors and managers in industry and commerce (class II). However, this order varies according to age-group. Apart from certain occupations which involve risks — miners, fishermen, steeplejacks, etc. — the variations in the mortality of occupational groups probably result more from the living conditions and modes of life than from occupational risks. This has been deduced from mortality data of wives. In any case, such risks cannot be accurately inferred from data of occupational mortality because of changes and mis-statements of occupation and because some occupations attract healthier persons. Living conditions are certainly highly influential in the patterns of mortality in Britain, not only general mortality but also by category of cause of death.

Catastrophic environmental factors, like floods, earthquakes and volcanoes, have caused abrupt loss of life, but more important is the influence of climate, and its intricate relationship with disease. We have only to look at the seasonal variations in mortality in Britain, where January deaths may be nearly twice those of August, for an indication of climatic effects, but these variations are diminishing. Factors such as climatic variability, insolation, aspect, atmospheric pollution, air conditioning and central heating all greatly affect health and mortality. It is a pity that climatic factors are so difficult to isolate. We should also recall the effects of solar and atomic radiations; it is clear that exposure to ionizing radiations increases the risk of developing leukaemia. Moreover, soils and the quality and quantity of water supply may be influential.

Causes of Death

Here we approach another contact-point — this time with medical geography, into which we must avoid major encroachment. Geographical studies of causes of death have been impeded in all but the most advanced countries by deficiencies in data. The reasons include the effectiveness of medical services, imperfect declarations of cause of death (too often the terms "senility" and "causes unknown" are used), lack of diagnosis of large proportions of the population, as well as inadequate and varied nomenclatures and classifications of causes of death. WHO's *Manual of the International Statistical Classification of Diseases, Injuries and Causes of Death* has helped to produce more uniformity in classification, but there are still great difficulties in international comparison. Other problems also occur. For simplicity of registration and analysis, a single cause of death is given, when a person may be suffering from many ailments — but should the cause noted be the immediate cause or the long-term cause? Moreover, some causes of death have only been recently diagnosed, and were formerly unknown — influenza was only recognized in the 1880s. So historical comparisons may be hazardous.

There are two major groups of causes of death, namely those which are *degenerative*, or due to the gradual exhaustion of the body, and those which are *environmental*, or due to infectious diseases, cataclysms, accidents, social conditions, etc. In countries where disease has been controlled, degenerative causes of death are preponderant — senility, heart diseases, vascular lesions and cancer — but where diseases are less controlled environmental causes hold sway. Another broad classification of human diseases differentiates between (a) diseases which are common in any climate and at any standard of living (e.g. chicken-pox, measles, mumps, pneumonia), (b) diseases associated with low standards of living, and (c) tropical diseases. The tropics seem to have harboured not only specifically tropical diseases but the other two groups as well.

In his syntheses on medical geography, Stamp has pointed out that mapping of mortality and disease has occurred at four distinct levels. At the world level the outstanding contribution has been by Jacques May, whose *Atlas of Diseases* and *Studies in Medical Geography* are fundamental. Stamp describes certain of the virulent diseases as "world killers", and the list is long: malaria, yellow fever, dengue, scarlet fever, measles, leprosy, scrub typhus, hookworms, tapeworms, tuberculosis, trachoma, influenza, dysentery, brucellosis, typhoid and paratyphoid, smallpox, syphilis, bronchitis, pneumonia, diabetes, poliomyelitis, plague, cancer and rheumatoid arthritis. Nobody examining the maps of distribution of disease could refrain from concluding that climate has a dominant role. This role is also prominent at the continental level, the second level referred to by Stamp, who examines the geographical distributions of diseases in Africa. Patterns of diseases in that continent are so closely related with population distribution, malnutrition and problems of cultivation that no relevant geographical study can ignore them. Learmonth's useful studies of the medical geography of India and Pakistan are at the subcontinental level.

The third level is the nation, and here a notable example is the *National Atlas of Disease Mortality*, prepared by Howe for the United Kingdom. The atlas includes maps of cancer (lung, stomach, breast and uterus), diseases of the circulatory system (arteriosclerotic heart disease and vascular lesions), diseases of the respiratory system (bronchitis, pneumonia and tuberculosis), diseases of the digestive system (gastric and duodenal ulcers), as well as other "miscellaneous" causes of death. A similar but smaller study was made by

Murray. The distinction between Highland Britain and Lowland Britain is apparent in many of the maps, particularly tuberculosis of the respiratory system, cancer of the stomach and vascular lesions affecting the central nervous system, with higher rates in the less-favoured parts of Highland Britain. On the other hand, lung cancer seems more prevalent in Lowland

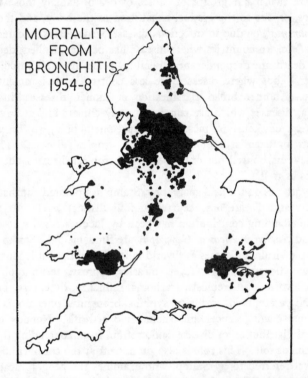

FIG. 21. Male mortality from bronchitis in England and Wales, 1954–8. Areas in black have above-average standardized mortality rates. Simplified from Howe, G. M., *National Atlas of Disease Mortality*, 1963. Bronchitis is mainly an urban disease, especially of industrial centres.

Britain, though like bronchitis (Fig. 21) and pneumonia it is primarily an urban disease.

The final level is the detailed local study, such as that done by Dr. Snow in the last century. One of the avowed aims of Stamp's *The Geography of Life and Death* is to stimulate geographers and general practitioners to do this sort of local research, to find out if the distributional patterns of disease and cause of death suggest correlations or causative factors.

References

BENJAMIN, B., *Social and Economic Factors affecting Mortality*, The Hague, 1965.

BROCKINGTON, F., *World Health*, 1958.

HOWE, G. M., The geographical distribution of cancer mortality in Wales, 1947–53, *Trans. and Papers Inst. Brit. Geographers*, **28**, 189 (1960).

HOWE, G. M., The geographical variation in disease mortality in England and Wales in the mid-twentieth century, *Advancement of Science*, 415 (Jan. 1961).

HOWE, G. M., *National Atlas of Disease Mortality*, 1963.

HOWE, G. M., A national atlas of disease mortality in the United Kingdom, *Geog. J.*, **130**, 15 (1964).

LEARMONTH, A. T. A., Medical geography in India and Pakistan, *Geog. J.*, **127**, 10 (1961).

MAY, J. M., *Studies in Medical Geography*, New York, 3 vols., 1958–61.

MAY, J. M., *Atlas of Diseases*, New York, 1950–5.

MURRAY, M. A., The geography of death in England and Wales, *Ann. Assoc. Amer. Geographers*, **52**, 130 (1962).

MURRAY, M. A., The geography of death in the United States and the United Kingdom, *Ann. Assoc. Amer. Geographers*, **57**, 301 (1967).

STAMP, L. D., *Some Aspects of Medical Geography*, 1964.

STAMP, L. D., *The Geography of Life and Death*, 1964.

STOLNITZ, G. J., Recent mortality trends in Latin America, Asia and Africa, *Population Studies*, **19**, 117 (1965).

U.N., *Population Bulletin*, No. 6 (1962).

CHAPTER IX

MIGRATIONS

The Mobility of Man

The mobility of man has increased fitfully with technical and economic progress. He has specialized means of transport to assist this mobility, so that distance is spoken of in terms of time according to the mode of transport. Increased mobility has enabled increased migrations. Unfortunately, there is no unanimity over the meaning of this latter term, though many consider it as movements involving a change of residence of substantial duration. On these grounds of definition we should exclude the constant movement of pastoral nomads, the temporary movement of tourists and the daily movement of commuters, but there can be little justification for their exclusion merely because we have no satisfactory term which encompasses the numerous spatial movements of populations. In this chapter we shall therefore consider, albeit briefly, a wider range of movements than is normally dealt with under such a heading.

Classification and Terminology

The extreme diversity of migrations in cause, duration, distance, direction, volume, velocity, selectivity and organization prohibits simple classification. We read of seasonal, temporary, periodic and permanent migrations, of spontaneous, forced, impelled, free and planned migrations, as well as of internal, external, inter-regional, international, continental and inter-continental migrations. Obviously no typology satisfactorily incorporates all types of human migration, and the problem is exacerbated by the lack of uniformity in terminology. It is not surprising that there is a growing tendency to consider migrations as either internal (within a state) or external (international). This approach has been induced by the great significance of state boundaries and the availability of data at the state level. Such a simple distinction cannot satisfy geographers who are interested not merely in numerical gains and losses due to migrations and their demographic, social and economic effects, but also in environmental influences upon migration streams and consequences in areas of departure and destination.

It would be unwise to consider that internal and external migrations are entirely different in causes, characteristics and consequences, though they

130

have influenced terminology. By emigration and immigration we mean departure from or entry into a state for the purpose of changing residence. These are usually termed permanent when the residence is for more than one year, and temporary when it is for less. The distinction between a temporary immigrant and a visitor is clear in theory but not in practice, for a visitor may be defined as a non-resident intending to remain for one year or less without engaging in an occupation within the country. But the intention as to the duration of migration may change on arrival. George has also noted various confusions in the terms emigration and immigration, which do not include, for example, migrations to and from colonial territories or between national groups within one state.

When we are considering internal migrations, the equivalent terms of emigration and immigration are out(ward)-migration and in(ward)-migration. Net external or internal migration is merely the balance and is often only a small fraction of gross migration, to which it may bear little relation. Migration rates relate the number of migrants to the population exposed to the likelihood of migrating, and may be specific for age and sex.

Differential Migration

Migrations are selective, and by differential migration we mean the tendency for certain elements of the population to be more migratory than others. Obviously migration streams vary a great deal in their selectivity according to the character and degree of specialization of the stream as well as the stage of its evolution, but on the whole migration is selective of people having a certain combination of traits rather than an individual trait.

The most-accepted migration differential is certainly that of age, for in both internal and external migrations late adolescents and young adults are usually preponderant, often migrating to their first job. Fortunately, they adjust themselves more easily to their new environments than do other age-groups. But even this generalization breaks down in some instances, where migration streams are composed of older adults and old people (e.g. migrations to retirement).

In Chapter VI there was discussion of the sex-selective effects of migration, noting the differences between advanced and underdeveloped countries and the historical changes in selection. Bold generalizations are that in advanced countries short-distance internal migrants are predominantly female while long-distance internal migrants are predominantly male; on the other hand, in many underdeveloped countries both internal and international migrants are predominantly male.

The marital status of migrants has also changed in developed countries. At one time migrants were mainly single — they are still so today in under-developed countries — but now there is more and more migration of families, looking for better houses, schools, social conditions and jobs. Consequently, family size is a selective factor of migration.

Migration is also more common among certain occupation groups than others. Professional classes are proportionally more migratory than either skilled or unskilled workers. Unemployed persons tend to be more migratory than employed persons. Migratory selection also takes place by race, nationality and educational attainment, and in general the process of selection depends more upon conditions at the destination than upon those at the place of origin, for migration which has a strong push stimulus tends to be less selective than migration which is mainly responsive to pull factors. As ethnic diversity, for example, is commonly associated with specialization of occupations and variations in socio-economic status (e.g. West Indians and Irish in Britain) as well as social segregation, the destination of such migrants is quite circumscribed.

1. INTERNAL MIGRATIONS

Measurement

Direct measurement of internal migration on a national scale is only possible in countries where a migration question is posed at the census or where there is a system of residence registration. This is the only satisfactory basis for calculating the volume and direction of migration streams. Alternatively, indirect measurements are possible:

(a) by comparison of two good consecutive censuses, either by the "vital statistics method", which estimates the total net gain or loss in population of a community as a result of migration by subtracting total net natural increase from total intercensal change; or by the "survival ratio method", which estimates the proportion of the population which should be expected to survive at the second census and determines the difference between this surviving expected population and the actual population; and

(b) by comparison of place-of-birth statistics with present residence.

The disadvantages of these methods are that we do not know when the migrations occurred, the number of moves made and the effect of mortality upon the migrants. We are sometimes compelled to supplement data by sample surveys.

Causes and Characteristics

The geographer finds himself at home in the study of migrations, for there are no laws. The causes are varied and complementary, and involve both "push" and "pull" factors both at origin and destination of migrants, which may defy simple distinction. Bogue lists 25 migration-stimulating situations for persons, 15 factors in choosing a destination, and 10 socio-economic conditions which can stimulate or retard mobility among a population. They are well worthy of summary.

(1) *Migration-stimulating conditions:*
Graduation; marriage; lack of marriage; employment offers; employment opportunities or bonanzas; migratory work; special skills; transfer of employment; sale of business; loss of farm; discharge from employment; low wages; retirement; death of relative; military service; medical care; imprisonment; political, racial or religious oppression; natural disasters; invasion or infiltration by outsiders; inheritance; maladjustment to community; wanderlust; social rejection; forced movement.

(2) *Factors in choosing destination:*
Cost of moving; presence of relatives or friends; living with them; employment offer; physical attractiveness of community; physical environment; amenities; population composition; special employment facilities; familiarity or knowledge; special assistance; subsidies; information; reputation; lack of alternative destinations.

(3) *Socio-economic conditions affecting migration:*
Major capital investments; major business recessions or fluctuations; technological change; changes in economic organization; provisions for social welfare; migration propaganda facilities; regulations affecting migration; living conditions and levels; tolerance of minorities of all types; migration policy.

These lists are not exhaustive. Other factors may be added like population pressure and growth, the availability of land in areas of departure and destination, transportation facilities, war, harvests, cultural differences and similarities. Geographers would also wish to include climatic and vegetational changes, fluctuations and contrasts, which have stimulated so many migrations from primitive pastoralism to the migrations for retirement. We should also add the factor of distance, with which the volume of migrations tends to vary inversely; this is known as the inverse distance law, expounded by Zipf. However, it has been postulated, by Stouffer, that the number of persons migrating a given distance is directly proportional to the number of opportunities at that distance and inversely proportional to the number of intervening opportunities; he later introduced another variable — competing migrants at destination. The size of a country is also relevant. Large countries encourage internal migrations; small countries often have no alternative to external migrations, which incur more social difficulties. We should also stress the effects of natural barriers, routes and regions on migration streams; the canalizing effects of some environmental features (e.g. the loessial belt of Europe) and the restraining effects of others (e.g. mountains, deserts).

It is not easy to assess the relative influences of the complex of factors affecting the decision of the migrant, and the decision to migrate is not necessarily rational — indeed many migrants, especially wives and children, do not actually take the decision. Migration streams are sensitive to constantly changing stimuli, yet they have also a certain inertia and sometimes reflect the influence of former distributive forces. It is also true that certain communities are prone to migration, and that areas of high in-migration (e.g. large cities) generally experience high out-migration. The mobility of the population of the United States is so great that every year one in five change their home, and about one-quarter do not live in the state where they were born.

Certainly, we should not imagine that migration is a one-way process; every migration stream has a counter-stream. Many migrants intend to stay at the places of destination only temporarily, many re-evaluate the "pull" factors at destination and many earn enough to return to their place of origin. But the counter-stream is not very large if there are many "push" factors from the place of origin, as for example from the Western Isles of Scotland. Similarly it tends to be small if the intervening obstacles are severe.

Seasonal Migrations

Many censuses distinguish between sedentary (stable) and nomadic populations. While we cannot consider in detail the modes of life of nomadic peoples, we must at least note causes and terms.

At the base of the economic scale are the nomadic food gatherers, who live by hunting, fishing or collecting and frequently engage in seasonal migrations. These peoples are generally relic peoples, close to nature, small in stature, with few material possessions, yet complex social structures and rites. They are located in small social groups with sparse densities either in remote corners of the earth (e.g. Tierra del Fuegians, Andamanese, Eskimos, reindeer hunters of Siberia) and/or hostile environments, especially tropical forests (e.g. Pygmies, Semang and Sakai of Malaysia, Veddas).

Pastoral nomadism is the movement of human groups and their flocks or herds following the distribution of pastures. It is found mainly in deserts, semi-deserts and extensive grasslands, though over a wide range of latitude. The character of nomadic societies, the size of nomadic groups, the distances, duration and direction of migrations, and the type of livestock (camels, cattle, goats, sheep, horses, reindeer) vary greatly with environmental conditions and traditions, so that there is a wide gamut of modes of life between pure nomadism and a completely sedentary existence. A common distinction is between nomadism and semi-nomadism, on the basis of the time given each year to cultivation. True nomads often own trees or farms in oases or mountain villages, but they do not work the land themselves; semi-nomads devote a considerable time to cultivation and are sedentary for part of each year. They inhabit principally the desert fringes, and are usually more numerous than true nomads. Both nomads and semi-nomads experience a rhythmic migratory existence closely attuned to seasonal climatic changes. We think of the Persian nomads (e.g. Kashgai) who migrate between the Zagros mountains and the Persian Gulf coasts, the Saharan nomads (e.g. Arbaa) who move into the Algerian *tell* in summer, and the seasonal movements of Sudanese cattle breeders (e.g. Baggara).

Nomadic pastoralists are rarely found in dense concentrations, but cover a considerable proportion of the earth's surface, especially in the Old World. In contact with modern societies they have frequently suffered through (a) the introduction of modern transport which has reduced the caravan trade, (b) military or police security which has reduced raiding and "protection" of less warlike groups, and (c) agricultural developments which have encroached on their pastures. Nomads have often been treated as an anachronism by new states, and have sometimes been forcibly settled. By spontaneous, planned or forced settlement their numbers are likely to diminish.

Seasonal pastoral migrations need not entail nomadism. When flocks moving between widely separated pasture zones are accompanied only by herders, either wage-earners or members of the family owning the flocks, we term the movement transhumance. Typical of mountainous Mediterranean environments, where sheep pasture valleys in winter and mountains in summer, it may be ascendant (if practised by valley dwellers), descendant (by mountain dwellers) or double (by peoples on mountain slopes). While on the wane in the Mediterranean, transhumance is replacing nomadism on the desert fringes of the Maghreb.

Both nomadism and transhumance frequently involve commercial transactions and seasonal employment in harvesting. Harvests stimulate migrations in many parts of the world, especially where commercial cultivation is practised. In Europe, fruit and hop picking, potato gathering, and the grain, olive and grape harvests have long attracted migrant labourers, though mechanical methods are reducing their numbers for some crops. Yet even in the United States we find teams of migrant wheat harvesters who move with their combines from Texas in June to Manitoba in September, and similar northward migrations of harvesters of sugar-beet and fruit. Indeed, the size and climatic variety of the country permit constant migration of agricultural labourers to planting and harvesting.

Other industries like fishing, fish-canning, fruit-canning, alluvial diamond mining, tourism and entertainment also have a seasonal character and involve migration of labour. Pilgrimages are also important seasonal migration streams; those to Lourdes, Mecca and Benares involve many hundreds of thousands each year.

Periodic Migrations

Many migrants remain away from their permanent homes for periods of a few years and return periodically. The main aim of the majority of these periodic (or temporary) migrants is to earn enough to send home remittances for the family and to establish themselves in better circumstances on their return. Millions of migrant labourers in Africa are of this type: the north-south movements in West Africa; the movements in East and Central Africa to Nairobi, Buganda, the sisal areas of Tanzania and the Copperbelt; the movements to the mines and industries of South Africa; and the movements to the mines and towns of the Maghreb. Many of the migrants from oases and villages of the northern Sahara engage in small specialized occupations (grocers, porters, doughnut-sellers, newspaper-sellers, dockers) in the towns, and some villages managed to exercise almost a monopoly of a certain occupation. Periodic migrants are sometimes tempted to settle permanently in their place of work, despite initial intentions of remaining there only temporarily. The blandishments of towns exert a strong hold.

Another form of periodic migration is the farm-to-farm migration associated with the systems of tenancy and share-cropping. New Year's Day is "moving day" on the plantation districts in the southern part of the United States. Bush-fallowing in the tropics is another type. It entails the cultivation of a patch of land for a period of years until the soils show signs of exhaustion. Then the patch is abandoned to natural regeneration, after which it may be used again. Bush-fallowing is often associated with the movement of villages, but rarely with dense populations.

Rural–Urban, Urban–Rural and Intra-urban Migrations

Migrations from rural to urban areas are generally the most important form of internal migration, especially in countries experiencing industrialization and rapid technological change, where they have played a major role in economic development and the rise of *per capita* incomes. In the United States, for example, the great bulk of internal migrations are towards the towns or their suburbs, whether the migrations are between counties, states or regions. The same is true in the U.S.S.R. But in highly urbanized countries, like Britain, rural–urban migrations are being replaced by inter-urban and urban–rural migrations.

Rural–urban migrations are primarily a response to economic motives. In the areas of departure, population pressure, modernization of agriculture (especially the mechanization and methods of commercial production), as well as the traditional systems of land tenure have been key "push" factors, while the rapid increase of employment opportunities (often with better working conditions) in urban areas is the major "pull". The role of transport facilities, especially the railways, in breaking down traditional rural isolation has been primordial in many parts of the world. They have increased cultural contacts and made known the availability of employment; cultural contrasts still inhibit internal migrations in some countries, like India. Employment opportunities are also influenced by business cycles (depressions are invariably accompanied by immobility of population) as well as by the slower natural increase of population in many urban areas. On the whole, rural–urban migration involves the less fortunate, and in advanced countries, at least, it has been beneficial in correcting labour surpluses and unemployment in rural areas. Many rural–urban migrants are taking up their first employment, but others are changing their occupation often from an agricultural to a non-agricultural one. This fundamental mutation in occupational structure is one of the main results of rural–urban migration. The main employment attractions are factories, shops, offices, building and public services.

Towns also offer seductive amenities: schools, shops, public utilities, entertainments. The inconveniences — costs of living, housing and transport, noise, atmospheric pollution — are often realized only too late. The influx has often posed severe moral and social problems and great housing difficulties. Slums and shanty-towns are often symptomatic of maladjustments arising from rural–urban migration. And not all migrants have jobs to go to. In order to reduce the numbers of beggars and unemployed in the towns, some countries (e.g. Italy) have at one time or another required migrants to possess certificates of employment.

In rural areas the effects of migration may vary from a welcome relief from population pressure to depopulation, dereliction and abandonment. Between these two extremes lie various stages, such as the adverse effects of unbalanced age and sex-structures on farming, population growth and social activities, the closure of village schools, the retreat from marginal hill land, the amalgamation of properties. . . . The worst-affected localities are generally those with difficult physical conditions: mountain villages, remote islands, oases.

In some countries small towns act as intermediate stations for the flow of rural–urban migrants, but stepped migration is not a universal feature. Many of the small towns, suburbs and rural areas within commuting range of large cities are growing more rapidly than the cities themselves. The drift out from the centres of large cities is associated with the growing land values there and the improvements in transportation. A century ago, well over 100,000 people lived in the city of London; today there are only 5000, mostly watchmen and caretakers. Both the "inner ring" and the "suburban ring" are losing migrants while the "Green Belt ring" and "outer country ring" are gaining them. Sponsored migration to new towns has assisted the centrifugal movement, which is a common feature of large cities, especially of developed countries. The 1961 census of England and Wales revealed that many are experiencing a decline in population: Liverpool, Manchester, Newcastle, Sheffield, Derby, Leicester, Stoke, Wolverhampton.

A major factor in intra-urban migration decisions is place utility, which has been defined by Simmons as a measure of attractiveness or unattractiveness of an area, relative to alternative locations, as perceived by the decision-maker. In residential movement aspirations of the household with respect to housing and the availability of vacant houses are instrumental factors.

Journey to Work and Leisure

The above process is closely connected with the growth of journey to work. The economies in the large-scale concentration of industries and commerce have provoked a dispersal of residences, permitted by the increased facilities of travel. The separation of workplace and residence incurs journeys to work which, as Lawton has stated, are "an expression of dissonance". Moreover, they are expensive, time-consuming and exhausting, and can never be eliminated. Something, however, can be done by improving transport facilities and planning.

It is unfortunate that censuses often give only bare indications of journey to work. Even the available census data in England and Wales is recorded only in terms of local authority areas, with no information about length or duration of journeys. One interesting technique, devised by Westergaard, is the mapping of *job ratios*, which are the ratios between the occupied resident population (the "night population") of a district with the working population ("day population") multiplied by 100. Indices over 100 indicate an excess of jobs over resident workers.

Patterns of journeys to work are complex, and many causes can be distinguished:

(1) the practice of part-time smallholding and part-time industrial employment, and the employment of farm-dwellers in urban activities;

(2) the desire of many urban workers to live in rural or semi-rural surroundings;

(3) the inadequacy and high costs of housing in urban areas;

(4) functional segregation within urban areas of residential areas and industrial/administrative/commercial/cultural quarters;

(5) the variety of occupations within a given community and the scatter of workplaces, in particular the differences in the occupational structure of the male and female working populations.

Consequently, routes of movement are intricate. In large cities they may be radial, circumferential or transverse. The real problem is the congestion on a few routes at rush hours. The latter vary slightly from country to country, and necessitate special transport arrangements which may not be used at other times.

Week-ends and holiday seasons, however, present the special features of travel to leisure. This phenomenon, associated with urbanization and rising standards of living, is most common in developed countries. Travel may last from a few hours on a Saturday afternoon to a few months in summer, and may involve a few miles or a few thousand. Travel for leisure in developed countries means vast movements of population and has major influences upon regional economies and population distribution.

Inter-regional Migrations

Inter-regional migrations cannot be easily dissociated from rural–urban migrations. Indeed, most recent inter-regional migrations have been from rural and urban areas of one region to urban areas of another.

There is no space here to deal with the numerous types of inter-regional movement, but we should like to emphasize two, namely, colonizing migrations and general drifts of population. Colonizing migrations may be spontaneous or planned. The move west in nineteenth-century America was largely spontaneous, though the railway companies had a great part in organizing it and the government in encouraging it. The movement still continues, especially to California, but there is a growing counter-migration. The move east in Russia was also greatly assisted by the Trans-Siberian Railway, but became more planned after 1925. Since then, migrants have gone more to towns than to rural areas. After the Second World War, there was a movement in the opposite direction to the occupied countries in eastern Europe. The Great Trek of the Boers was another dramatic colonizing migration.

Drifts of population from one part of a country to another, from the less-favoured to the more-favoured regions, are widespread. In Britain, there is a general drift to the south, particularly the south-east. This movement is partly associated with the growth of London and its satellites and partly with the migration to retirement in the south. In Germany there is a general drift westward, accentuated by the great volume of refugees from East Germany. In the United States there are strong flows towards the north-east, especially of unskilled and semi-skilled negroes, the south-east and the west, emphasizing the peripheral distribution and, as in so many countries, accentuating the unevenness of population distribution.

2. INTERNATIONAL MIGRATIONS

International migrations are of greater demographic significance than internal migrations, as they mean either a gain or a loss in a country's population. In most countries natural increase exceeds the net gain by migrations, yet modern governments make far greater efforts to regulate and control migrations than ever they do to influence fertility. Despite this, statistics of international migration are notoriously poor. We can only adequately assess the effects of migration on the population-structure and labour force of sending and receiving countries if data differentiate between long-term (permanent) and short-term (temporary) migrants, visitors and residents, and are classified according to age, sex and marital status, preferably for nationals and aliens separately. Generally the wide diversity of tabulations of international migration data makes comparisons very difficult. Another great problem about international migrations is assessing their future volume; migrations are the main unknown component of population projections and estimates.

Determinants

Many of the determinants of international migrations are the same as for internal migrations, especially the economic motives. Studies of annual oscillations in nineteenth-century migration between Europe and North America have shown correlations with harvests in countries of origin and with business cycles and pace of economic development especially in receiving countries. Yet statements about economic motives can rarely remain unqualified. The contrasting standards of living of sending and receiving countries have encouraged migration streams — but countries with extremely low standards of living are rarely rich sources of migrants, and economic opportunities may attract migrants from rich to poor countries. The contrasting availability of land in countries of emigration and immigration has also encouraged peoples to migrate — yet land is no longer a key attraction, and the mere existence of unoccupied land has not been always enough to attract immigrants. Similarly, it is difficult to generalize about the influence of industrialization in sending and receiving countries upon emigration and immigration.

Demographic factors are general determinants. Population pressure helps to explain a great deal about international migrations. It was the stimulus of emigration from Ireland in the nineteenth century (though famine was the trigger), and from Italy and south-east Europe in the late nineteenth and early twentieth centuries. It is the main stimulus of emigration from a number of islands and small countries, like Malta, Corsica, Rwanda, Burundi, Puerto Rico, Trinidad, Aden and The Netherlands. Some small countries almost specialize in emigration. The case of the Lebanon is illuminating. Only 4105 square miles in area with a population of 2·6 millions, it has exported 1,500,000 Lebanese all over the world (400,000 to the U.S.A., 350,000 to Brazil, 200,000 to Argentina, and many to West Africa). Most have given up their Lebanese nationality, but they have retained their links with their homeland and send back a proportion of their ample earnings as traders and bankers.

Demographic factors particularly influence migration policies, which affect external migration much more than internal migration. Policies have varied greatly. Few major countries, apart from Britain, Italy and Japan, have actively encouraged emigration, and some have severely restricted it, including pre-war Germany and Italy, the U.S.S.R. and East European countries. Immigration policies have been more important. In the nineteenth century there was greater freedom of entry than there is today. While some immigrant countries, like Australia, provide financial assistance to immigrants, these immigrants are selected. And most of the restrictive immigration measures passed by the great immigrant countries of the last century have qualitative as well as quantitative dispositions designed to restrict the entry of certain ethnic groups which are considered undesirable. The White Australia Policy, the quota systems of the United States which have operated in favour of north-west Europeans rather than south or east Europeans, the small quotas of Chinese permitted entry into South-East Asian countries, the restrictions on coloured immigrants into Britain ... there are many examples of planned selective immigration. In New Zealand, trade unions have seen immigration as a threat to wages, and have been influential in policy-making. Restrictions on immigration into Latin America have been fewer and more recent.

International migration seems to be more and more influenced by political factors, and less a matter of individual choice. There have been massive exchanges of population, as between Greece and Turkey during the years 1923–33 and between Rumania and Bulgaria after 1940. Migrations have taken place in the face of invading armies, as in Russia and China, and millions have migrated as forced labourers, displaced persons or prisoners. International organizations like the International Labour Organization (ILO) and the United Nations Relief and Rehabilitation Administration (UNRRA) have assisted the movements of peoples, especially refugees, in many parts of the world. Political refugees in Europe are now numbered in tens of millions, and when partition occurred in the Indian sub-continent millions moved to

be with their co-religionists. Religion is still a potent influence, as we see with
the Jewish migrations to Israel.

Consequences

The consequences of international migrations are not unlike those of
internal migrations, especially the changes in age, sex and economic compositions in sending and receiving countries. These effects are heightened in
countries of Asia and Africa where migrants are mainly male. In small
densely populated underdeveloped countries, emigration may act as a safety
valve and assist economic development. Even in Italy it reduced unemployment, raised the general standard of living, and developed maritime trade and
transport. But in the larger populous countries of Asia it has little overall
effect. In sparsely populated underdeveloped countries, immigration has
meant many things, including a stimulus to internal migrations; the establishment of European colonists, acceptable (South America) or otherwise (Africa),
and an administrative class; the growth of an alien trading class, like the
Indian, Chinese and Syrian/Lebanese traders; and a migratory labour force,
like the miners in Africa.

International migrations also influence wage rates, unemployment, *per
capita* output, standards of living and the balance of international payments,
but all are affected by so many other factors that it is hard to isolate the
influence of migrations. Particular cases may be highly suggestive, but
contradictory evidence is often available from other sources. Equally, it is
impossible to be dogmatic about the social consequences of international
migrations. It is true that immigrants often feel fewer roots, have less social
conscience and are less law-abiding than residents, but much depends upon
their integration and absorption into community life. Consequently, receiving
countries usually favour the dispersion of immigrants of particular nationalities
rather than their natural tendency to congregate.

Recent International Migrations

The great trans-oceanic migrations from Europe during the nineteenth and
early twentieth centuries were the most spectacular ever known. Europe
replaced Asia as the reservoir of mankind and opened its ducts to the Americas,
Australasia and parts of Africa. The movement developed after 1815, when
the emigrants were mainly from the soaring populations of industrializing
north-west Europe and from overpopulated rural Ireland, going mainly to
North America. Although emigration from these countries increased through
the century, towards the end it was surpassed by more massive emigration
from countries of rural overpopulation in southern and eastern Europe.
Whereas about 17 millions left the United Kingdom between 1825 and 1920
(65 per cent to the U.S.A., 15 to Canada, 11 to Australia, 5 to South Africa,

and 4 to other destinations), that same number left Italy between 1880 and 1914, although only one-third were permanent emigrants. The main move was between 1901 and 1910, when 5·9 millions left Italy, 3·4 the Austro-Hungarian Empire, 2·8 Great Britain and 1·6 France. The United States was, of course, the greatest recipient of all these migrants and between 1840 and 1914 received 50 millions, 40 millions of whom came between 1880 and 1914.

After the First World War there was a rapid decline of overseas migrations from Europe, for many reasons: immigration and emigration restrictions, financial chaos in Europe, the world crisis of 1929, declining natural increase, the introduction of unemployment and health assistance, the reduction in the amount of new land overseas, and the greater desire of overseas countries for skilled workers than for unskilled labourers. Indeed, during the thirties some of the countries of western Europe, like France, Britain and Germany, were gaining more migrants than they lost. France, in particular, received millions of immigrants from neighbouring countries and from Poland, and they helped to fill gaps caused by the First World War and provided a useful labour force for the mines and factories.

Tens of millions were displaced during the Second World War, especially in Europe and China, and many have never returned to their former homes. Partitions of Germany and India have also caused massive migrations — at least 10 millions moved between India and Pakistan. A smaller but substantial number of Jews have fled to Israel, where they displaced many of the indigenous Arabs.

Displaced persons and refugees have contributed to the recrudescence of overseas migrations. In the first seven post-war years 4,452,000 persons emigrated from Europe, while 1,150,000 were immigrants. Emigrants from Britain, Germany and The Netherlands have gone to Australia, New Zealand, the U.S.A. and Canada. Italians and Spaniards have gone mostly to South America, though Italians are numerous in Britain and all the Common Market countries. Australia, in particular, has welcomed migrants from many European countries, especially family units, skilled tradesmen and white-collar workers, increasingly from countries other than the U.K. Between 1947 and 1961, 1,500,000 migrants and their Australian-born children were added to the population, 32 per cent from the U.K. and Dominions (compared with 90 per cent of the net immigrants between 1901 and 1921), 27 per cent from southern Europe, 20 per cent from eastern Europe and 18 per cent from northern Europe. In consequence, the non-British element of the Australian population reached 9·3 per cent in 1961, in contrast to only 2 per cent in 1947.

Northern and western Europe have become important competing areas for migrants, but for workers more than for family units. Immigration has contributed considerably to the revival of population growth in France, for she has received not only immigrants from various European countries, but also more than a million of her nationals from former colonial territories, especially Algeria, Morocco and Tunisia, as well as several hundred thousand nationals of these newly independent territories.

International migrations from and within Europe have lost the spontaneity common in the nineteenth century. They have a more political flavour. But Europe is still the main source of international migrants. In comparison, migrations from Asia have been small, especially considering the immense populations of that continent. In 1963 it was estimated that 30 million Chinese had settled outside of Mainland China, but the communist régime has arrested much of the flow. Between 1834 and 1937 the net outward migration from India was only 6 millions, mostly to other parts of the Indian Ocean community, especially as indentured labourers, but Indians abroad now number only about 5 millions. However, discriminatory immigration restrictions severely limit possibilities of emigration from Asiatic countries to other parts of the world, so the population problems of these countries must be solved internally.

Finally, mention must be made of international tourist flows which have increased massively since the Second World War, especially with the advent of jet-flight "packaged" holidays, as for example from north-west Europe to Mediterranean resorts. Principal influences are distance, cost, climate and touristic appeal.

References

BOGUE, D. J., Internal Migration, in *The Study of Population*, ed. by HAUSER, P. M. and DUNCAN, O. D., Chicago, 1959.

DICKENSON, R. E., The geography of commuting: the Netherlands and Belgium, *Geog. Review*, **47**, 521 (1957).

HAGERSTRAND, T., Migration and area, in D. Hannerberg *et al.* (Eds.), *Migration in Sweden—a symposium*, Lund Studies in Geography, 1957.

ISAAC, J., *Economics of Migrations*, 1947.

ISAAC, J., *British Post-War Migration*, 1954.

JACKSON, J. A. (Ed.), *Migration*, 1969.

JANSEN, C. J. (Ed.), *Readings in the Sociology of Migration*, 1970.

JOHNSTON, R. J., A reconnaissance study of population change in Nidderdale, *Trans. and Papers Inst. Brit. Geographers*, **41**, 113 (1967).

KARIEL, H. G., Selected factors areally associated with population growth due to net migration, *Ann. Assoc. Amer. Geographers*, **53**, 210 (1963).

LAWTON, R., The daily journey to work in England and Wales, *Town Planning Review*, **29**, 241 (1959).

LAWTON, R., The journey to work in England and Wales, *Tijdschrift voor Economische en Sociale Geografie*, **54**, 61 (1963).

LEE, E. S., A theory of migration, *Demography*, **3**, 47 (1966).

LOWENTHAL, D. and COMITAS, L., Emigration and depopulation: Some neglected aspects of population geography, *Geog. Review*, **52**, 195 (1962).

MABOGUNJE, A. L., Systems approach to a theory of rural–urban migration, *Geographical Analysis*, **2**, 1 (1970).

NEWTON, M. P. and JEFFERY, J. R., *Internal Migration: Some Aspects of Population Movements within England and Wales*, 1957.

OLSSON, G., Distance and human interaction: a migration study, *Geografiska Annaler*, B, **47**, 3 (1965).

PROTHERO, R. M., Continuity and change in African population mobility, *Geographers and the Tropics: Liverpool Essays*, ed. by STEEL, R. W. and PROTHERO, R. M., 189 (1964).

PROTHERO, R. M., *Migrants and Malaria*, 1965.

ROSE, A. J., The geographical pattern of European immigration in Australia, *Geog. Review*, **48**, 512 (1958).

SAVILLE, J., *Rural Depopulation in England and Wales, 1851–1951*, 1957.

SIMMONS, J. W., Changing residence in the city: a review of intra-urban mobility, *Geog. Review*, **58**, 622 (1968).

SORRE, M., *Les Migrations des peuples: Essai sur la mobilité géographique*, 1955.

STOUFFER, S. A., Intervening obstacles: a theory relating mobility and distance, *Am. Sociological Review*, **5**, 845 (1940).

TAFT, D. R. and ROBBINS, R., *International Migrations: The Immigrant in the Modern World*, New York, 1955.

THOMAS, B., *Migration and Economic Growth*, 1954.

THOMAS, B. (Ed.), *The Economics of International Migration*, 1958.

U.N., Population Studies No. 5, *Problems of Migration Statistics*; No. 11, *Sex and Age of International Migrants: Statistics for 1918–1947*; and No. 12, *Economic Characteristics of International Migrations: Statistics for Selected Countries, 1918–1954*.

WILLIAMS, A. V. and ZELINSKY, W., On some patterns of international tourist flows, *Econ. Geog.*, **46**, 549 (1970).

CHAPTER X

POPULATION GROWTH

THE reason for calling this chapter "Population Growth" rather than "Population Change" is that at national level very few populations are declining. Most are growing so rapidly that world population growth is one of the major problems of the present. On the other hand, within developed countries there are usually many districts experiencing population decline.

Measures of Population Growth and Replacement

Apart from the absolute increase or decrease per annum, one of the most common measures of growth is the *annual rate of increase*. The U.N. Demographic Yearbooks use the following formula:

$$\left(\sqrt[t]{\frac{P_1}{P_0}} \; - 1 \right) \times 100$$

where P_0 is the population at the beginning of the period, P_1 is the population at the end of the period, and t is the number of years. The two main components may be census returns or population estimates, and so the rate is subject to the general qualifications for such data. It is a useful rate, and may be helpful in assessing the accuracy of vital and migration statistics.

Natural increase is the positive difference between the numbers of births and deaths, and the *natural increase rate* is the difference between the crude birth and death rates; natural decrease and *natural decrease rates* are negative differences, but they are less common, except in rural areas of developed countries. A natural increase rate may also be calculated by subtracting deaths from births and dividing by the population total for a specific year. Despite its widespread use, this rate expresses population growth very imperfectly, as it ignores the ageing of each individual during the year and does not differentiate between the deaths of old and young persons. In other words, natural increase rates ignore age-composition, so a population with a high proportion in the reproductive age-groups might have a positive natural increase rate and yet experience low fertility and lack of replacement. Similarly, a population with declining mortality might register an excess of

146

births over a long period although its fertility might not be high enough to ensure replacement. Eventually, however, the inevitability of death would reveal the true state of affairs. The point is that natural increase rates should be treated with caution.

Refinements have been proposed, but not widely used. Hersch, for example, suggested the *potential natural increase rate*:

$$\frac{(B \times E) - (D \times A)}{PL}$$

where B is the number of births, E the expectation of life at birth, D the number of deaths, A the average age of the deceased persons, and PL the life potential of the total population (i.e. the total number of years that the population has yet to live).

In studying population growth, many demographers have confined their attentions to closed or isolated populations, where there are no external additions or losses by migrations. In practice, closed populations are rare, but the approach helps in the understanding of vital processes. Lotka, for instance, examined the case of a closed population where fertility and mortality are constant, and showed how such a population tends towards a fixed age-structure. It would increase or decrease at a constant rate and in geometrical progression, although the age-structure would not change. Such a population is termed stable, and any accidental occurrence affecting mortality would tend to be corrected and evened out. A stationary population is one where fertility and mortality are equal, and everything becomes constant, with the age-structure identical to the survival table. In recent years the 'quasi-stable' population theory has been developed, especially by Coale and Bourgeois-Pichat, who have demonstrated that age distributions are not very sensitive to changes in mortality and can therefore provide information on fertility, even if little is known about mortality. This theory has been used to obtain demographic measures from broad age-compositions in developing countries where little other evidence is available.

Reproduction rates are related to the stable population. One of their aims is to enable comparisons through the computation of an index. The *gross reproduction rate* of Kuczynski is the sum of all the age-specific birth rates of women aged 15–49 divided by 1000 (i.e. the total fertility rate) and multiplied by the proportion of feminine births. In other words, it expresses how many girls would be born to a new-born girl during the course of her life supposing that she lived until 50 and supposing also no change in feminine fertility. When the gross reproduction rate equals one, there should be replacement of one generation by another; when it is less than one, this is impossible.

The *net reproduction rate* is a further refinement. Whereas the gross reproduction rate assumes no mortality before the age of 50, the net reproduction rate takes mortality into account. The calculation is the same, except that each age–specific birth rate is multiplied by the appropriate survival rate. It is an advance over the preceding rate, and was widely used in the 1930s, when it was felt that it showed the trend of the population. Indeed, it confirmed some of the alarm in western Europe about the decline in the rate of population growth. However, the net reproduction rate is only a method of allowing for the disturbing effects of an abnormal age-structure and does not show trends, because it is usually based on the fertility and mortality of a single year and because there may be considerable variations in (a) the proportion of young married couples, which would affect fertility rates, and (b) the fertility rates of married couples in general. To overcome problems arising from an abnormal composition of the married population by duration of marriage, one may calculate a *marriage–standardized reproduction rate*, which includes assumptions as to the number of women who would be married at each age and their marriage-duration specific fertility rates. The statistical labour is obviously great, and one main difficulty is whether to use marriage rates or proportions married. Another type of marriage–standardized reproduction rate may be produced from actual fertility rates of marriage cohorts, i.e. groups of married couples who were married in the same year.

So reproduction rates may be concerned with the extent to which either a crop of births reproduce themselves about 30 years later, or a crop of persons of marriageable age in a given year reproduce themselves. But despite many refinements, these reproduction rates only show current tendencies, not future trends. Indeed, they are never entirely satisfactory, as it is difficult to incorporate statistically both fundamental characteristics of the population, like proportions married and the total number of children born to a woman, and experience rates of the population, like marriage rates and fertility rates.

Veyret-Verner has proposed the concept of demographic vitality, by incorporating age-structure with fertility and mortality in a single index, the *index of vitality*:

$$\frac{\text{Fertility rate} \times \text{Percentage aged 20–40}}{\text{Crude death rate} \times \text{Old-age index}}$$

where the old-age index is the relation between the over-60 and under-20 age-groups. Three types are distinguished: indices over 8 (e.g. in 1956: Japan 15·98, Canada 14·71, Argentina 13·65), between 4 and 8 (U.S.A. 7·54, Italy 7·80, Bulgaria 6·36, Norway 5·89), and below 4 (Switzerland 3·80, France 3·33, U.K. 2·64, West Germany 2·24). It is a useful index for regional comparisons, but there is a danger that it might be taken to suggest future trends.

We may conclude this section on statistical methods by two observations. First, analysis of generations is much more important in the study of replacement than in the study of mortality, for in the latter conditions of life have affected generations differently as they have grown older. Moreover, death may take us at any time, while our reproductive lives are very short. Secondly, complicated analysis of fertility and reproduction needs better data than are usually available.

Population Projections

It will be apparent that we know little about the relative importance of the numerous forces influencing fertility, mortality and migrations, and that no simple explanations can be given as to the main reasons for past demographic growth. How much more difficult then to predict the future. Yet, estimates of future population growth are highly desirable to governments, institutions and companies, so demographers are called upon to make population forecasts and projections. The distinction between these two terms is rarely clear, but the former is often stated in social and economic terms and the latter in purely demographic terms.

Although population projections appear to be mathematically complicated, we should remember that the validity of mathematics depends on the validity of the basic assumptions. In this case the assumptions concern fertility, mortality, marriage and migration, and naturally most assumptions are that these components will be much the same in the future as they are at present. The main problem is estimating future trends in fertility, the major long-term determinant of population growth, and this is why most of the projections of advanced countries in the 1930s and 1940s were so inaccurate, because they assumed declining fertility. Mortality is generally more predictable than fertility, because for the short term, at least, assumptions may be based on age-composition; for the long term the generation approach is better. Most population projections also make the wise condition that there will be no major war. Any future progress in medicine is likely to reduce mortality of the aged, but as they are beyond the reproductive period the effects will not be cumulative. Like mortality, marriage rates are influenced by population-structure, and so marriage assumptions are not too difficult. On the other hand, migrations are an unknown component, highly influential in some countries and negligible in others, and often fluctuating substantially.

In general, a series of projections is prepared to reveal the effects of varied assumptions. For example, the Royal Commission on Population of the 1940s used five alternative fertility bases, two mortality bases, five sets of marriage rates and five sizes of net migratory movement to establish a comprehensive series of 16 population projections for Great Britain. In the main report only three were mentioned. The series of projections is not averaged; each is examined individually, and the reader is left to draw his own conclusions.

Although projections are often carried forward 100 years, they are usually intended for short-term analysis. No wonder that they are so prone to misinterpretation and misunderstanding.

It is also not surprising that many projections are inaccurate, even in countries where data are fairly reliable. The rapid increase of population in the United States has exceeded most expectations. In 1921 Pearl and Reed postulated a total of 190 millions by A.D. 2000, while the Census Bureau proposed a slightly lower figure; but this total was achieved by 1963. In 1932 Whelpton and Thompson suggested a maximum of 140 millions by about 1956, when in fact the total was just under 169 millions. The Scripps Foundation 1943 estimate for 1960 was between 148 and 156·5 millions, while in 1949 the Census Bureau forecast 160 millions for 1960; the total in that year was 179·3 millions. The main reason for inaccuracy was the under-estimation of fertility.

The inaccuracy of the world population projections made by United Nations' demographers in the 1950s may be accounted for by unexpected high population figures at first censuses and unexpected declines in mortality. Slight errors in present calculations mean errors of billions of people at the end of the century. United Nations projections of world population made in 1963 assuming declining fertility had high, medium and low variants according to the time at which fertility decline is assumed to commence, and the respective totals for the year 2000 were 6994, 6130 and 5448 millions.

Although population projections have no specifically geographical connection, the subject has been touched upon here merely to remind ourselves of the dangers of accepting wholeheartedly forecasts of population growth.

Population Theories

The examination of differential fertility and mortality showed how little is known of the main influences upon population growth. Consequently, theories of population growth have been proposed, trying to explain the main influences, especially with respect to fertility. Coontz has classified these theories into three categories: biological, cultural and economic.

Biological theories stress that the law regulating human population growth is basically the same as that regulating the growth of plants and animals — that demographic growth is not unique. This view has found different exponents in the last two centuries, relating fertility to nutrition and density. The Brazilian dietician De Castro, for example, postulated in his *Geography of Hunger* that there is an inverse relationship between protein intake and human fertility. With sweeping generalizations he correlated low productivity and high reproductivity to hunger, especially specific hungers of proteins, minerals or vitamins, and blamed colonialism for much of the appalling hunger in the world today. Pearl and Reed are best known for their mathematical representation of human population growth known as the logistic curve (first proposed by the Belgian Verhulst nearly a century earlier, in 1838). It is based on the assumption that there are cycles of population growth reflecting changes in the economic organization of society, each cultural epoch having a different cycle. One important point about the logistic curve is that the proportional rate of population increase actually falls continuously, a concept backed by the contention that population growth is regulated by density; increasing density is said to lower fertility. Evidence for this contention was drawn from experiments with fruit flies and yeast cells — not always relevant to human populations.

Cultural theories of population growth emphasize the importance of man's character and culture in influencing his fertility. To explain the declining fertility of advanced countries, particular stress has been placed on the influence of desires for higher social and economic status and for more luxuries and pleasures in life. These are closely associated with the rational mentality, which weighs the advantages and disadvantages of parenthood with more materialistic desires, as well as the rising status of women. Increased education and urbanization have also been invoked as determinants of fertility decline, but these are certainly not universally true. Moreover, poverty cannot always be correlated with high fertility and wealth with low fertility.

Economic theories of population growth emphasize the significance of economic relations in social change. Although there are substantial differences in the theses of, say, the neo-classical economists and Marxist–Leninist economists, there has been more or less general agreement that the demand for labour determines its supply. Fluctuations in fertility, migrations and geographical distribution of population are therefore looked upon essentially as responses to the demand for labour.

Attitudes to Population Growth

The diversity in theories of population growth results partly from differences in experience and attitudes. Broadly speaking, there are two main attitudes to population growth — for and against. Those fearing it are usually concerned with the standard of living of the individual, believing that the restriction of numbers would be to the advantage of all. They fear overpopulation and the "population explosion", and foresee "standing room only". Many hold that there is an optimum population above which there should be no increase, for fear of impoverishment. Unemployment and low wages are attributed to surplus population. In this group, sometimes called the pessimists, are many Protestants, Americans, individualists and conservatives. However, alarm about population growth is not new, for overpopulation has long been the norm.

The initiator of so much thought along these lines was the Reverend Thomas Malthus, who in 1798 first published his *Essay on the Principle of Population* in opposition to the Poor Laws, which were designed to assist the needy in parishes. Malthus was anxious about the constant tendency for mankind to increase more rapidly than the amount of food available. He suggested that the population, when unobstructed, tends to double every 25 years and grows (but not indefinitely) at a geometrical rate, while the means of subsistence even under excellent conditions can never increase more than arithmetically. Opposed to this principle of population were "private checks", like moral restraint, celibacy and chastity until the responsibilities of marriage could be accepted, and "destructive checks" such as war, poverty, pest, famine and excess of all sorts. So Malthus demonstrated that population could not realize its tendency to increase geometrically. Unfortunately, he has been badly misrepresented. Adopted by the liberal economists and middle classes of the nineteenth century, the gist of Malthusianism has been preserved in various guises. It should be noted, however, that the neo-Malthusian movement which arose in England and America towards the end of the nineteenth century was concerned entirely with the publication of birth control methods, which Malthus had considered a vice.

The other main attitude to population growth is more optimistic, believing that population will find its own level naturally. This so-called populationist camp also has heterogeneous elements: many communists, practising Catholics, idealists and some socialists. Some believe that population is the wealth of the state; others that the family is the basis of society. Most castigate the pessimistic camp for the immorality of its views and excessive individualism. Marx was particularly violent in his attacks, persuaded that overpopulation resulted more from the maldistribution of the means of subsistence within society rather than from an overall deficiency. Marxists have referred to Malthusians as cannibalistic. The type of populationism expounded in Nazi Germany and in Fascist Italy was different; it was a totalitarian response to declining fertility and emigration, and was motivated by expansionist aims.

During the 1960s there developed a fairly strong reaction to these "either–or" extremist views. The success of family-planning programmes in some of the underdeveloped countries encouraged a less pessimistic view among many in the West, and at the same time the declining or low birth rates in many communist countries are in sharp contrast to Marxist preachings. At the World Population Conference held in Belgrade in 1965 a more moderate view emerged which recognized the immediacy of a world population problem, but saw no simple universal solution.

Population Policies

Governments have often tried to influence population growth, but have nearly always been populationist. Only recently have we seen strongly anti-natal policies adopted by capitalist Japan and communist China, as well as by India, Pakistan, Ceylon, Korea, Taiwan, Egypt and eastern European countries.

Modern states, especially totalitarian states, can have a powerful influence over population growth, both through direct measures to affect fertility, mortality and migration, and indirectly through their general policy, especially the economic policy. Population policies tend to be most effective when they conform to general policies, but it is never easy to assess the real effectiveness of direct measures.

Measures favouring fertility include family allowances, marriage loans, prevention of sale of birth control appliances, illegality of abortion, and ante- and post-natal care, while anti-natal measures comprise the legalization of abortion, birth control propaganda and sterilization. France has adopted most measures to favour fertility, in an effort to offset its tendency to decline, but we cannot be sure whether they are responsible for the recent high level of fertility or whether this is a response to economic expansion — perhaps a little of both. Japan, on the other hand, is an excellent example of a country with an anti-natal policy. Populationist during the Second World War, Japan found herself suddenly reduced to her own frontiers and forced to harbour her returning soldiers and colonizers. Faced with intense overpopulation, Japan promulgated the "law of eugenic protection" of 28th June 1948, which legalized sterilization and abortion under certain conditions and encouraged contraception. Abortions have been especially numerous and in 1955 reached a peak of 50·2 per thousand women of childbearing age. Between 1947 and 1957 the birth rate descended from 34·3 per thousand to 17·3, and it now remains low. The death rate also declined sharply, and so the natural increase in 1962 was 9·5 per thousand compared with 19·7 in 1947. In China there have been great heart-searchings over the need for birth control, and some vacillation. Between 1953 and 1958 a birth control campaign was waged, but for the following four years it was relaxed. Since mid-1962 there has been another campaign, this time against early marriages.

One of the main developments in recent years has been the emergence of population policies in underdeveloped countries. India was the first to institute a policy to reduce population growth, in 1950, but by 1968 more than twenty underdeveloped countries, many of them very large, had accepted the principle of family-planning programmes.

There is much more unanimity about death control than about birth control. All countries are agreed on the necessity of prolonging human life and take active measures to combat disease, to improve sanitation and hygiene, and to care for the aged. But death control is forgotten in war, revolution and genocide, such as the Nazi killing of nearly 6 million Jews. Racism, nationalism and political ideologies are also responsible for most of the limitations imposed upon international migration. It is sad to record that controls on such migration have increased during this century.

World Population Growth

The present world population of 3600 millions is only a small proportion (about 4 per cent) of the 77,000 millions estimated to have lived on earth during the last 600,000 years. The spectacular quickening in population growth dates only from the middle of the seventeenth century (Fig. 22). Yet although data are unreliable, it seems that the annual rate of increase doubled between 1650 and 1850, doubled again by the 1920s, and has since doubled again. By 1970 it was 2·0 per cent per annum. The total population has more than doubled during this century, and during the 1950s alone it rose by one-fifth or nearly 500 millions — about the estimated total population in the mid-seventeenth century. The annual increase now exceeds 70 million persons. If the increase rate persists at its present level, the world population will be multiplied sixfold within 100 years, but if there is a continued rise in the annual rate of increase there may be several billion more people. Projections by the United Nations' demographers have been rather conservative, but it looks as if there will be between 5000 and 7000 million people on earth by A.D. 2000.

Population growth by continents is extremely varied. The greatest influence on world population growth has certainly been the increase in the number of Asians, who, even without the Asian population of Russia, have long constituted the majority of mankind. Their proportion is now increasing. The

TABLE 10.1. MEDIUM ESTIMATES OF WORLD POPULATION, 1750–2000
(numbers in millions)

	1750	1800	1850	1900	1950	1970	2000
WORLD	791	978	1262	1650	2515	3635	6130
DEVELOPING COUNTRIES		919	1088	1682	2580	4742
Asia (ex. Japan and U.S.S.R.)	468	600	770	881	1298	1953	3336
Africa	106	107	111	133	222	344	768
Latin America	16	24	38	74	162	283	638
DEVELOPED COUNTRIES			343	562	834	1055	1388
Europe (ex. U.S.S.R.)	125	152	208	296	392	462	527
U.S.S.R.	42	56	76	134	180	243	353
North America	2	7	26	82	166	228	354
Japan	30	30	31	44	83	103	122
Oceania	2	2	2	6	13	19	32

(Source: Mainly from J. D. DURAND, The modern expansion of world population, *Proc. American Philosophical Society*, **111**, 137 (1967).)

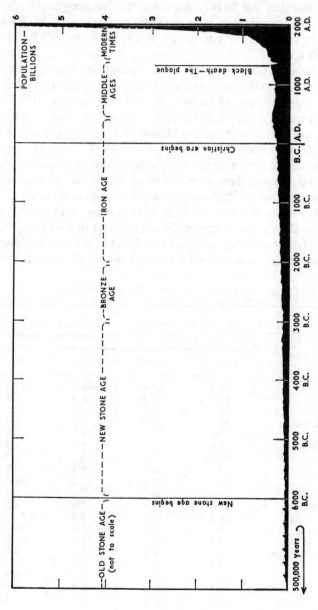

FIG. 22. The growth of world population. It has taken hundreds of thousands of years to reach 3000 millions, but the total may double by the end of this century. After DESMOND, A., in *The Population Crisis and the Use of World Resources*, ed. by MUDD, S., 1964.

Population Geography

numerical significance of Europe has also been great, but its rate of increase has dropped considerably during this century. The Americas and Africa both have an absolute increase far in excess of Europe (including the U.S.S.R.), and their combined populations have recently overtaken that of Europe. Although growing rapidly, the population of Oceania contributes little to world population growth.

During the 1950s the smallest annual rate of population increase (0·8 per cent) was in Europe, especially northern and western Europe, but the absolute increase of the continent was 64 millions, second only to Asia. The latter increased by 21 per cent or nearly 300 millions, about 60 per cent of the total world increase. The rate of increase was highest in South-West Asia, but the volume was much more impressive in South-Central and East Asia. Unfortunately, nobody can be sure about the population increase of China, which so heavily tips the balance. The same doubts are felt about the accuracy of the estimated increase of the African population, though there is no doubt about its rapidity. Latin America experienced even more rapid growth, and by the end of the decade had overtaken North America in total population. Oceania was the fastest-growing continent and the only one where migration had a considerable effect; it accounted for 30 per cent of the growth.

TABLE 10.2. POPULATION GROWTH BY REGIONS, 1920–60

	Decennial percentage increase		Percentage distribution of world population	
	1920–30	1950–60	1920	1960
WORLD TOTAL	11·3	19·3	100·0	100·0
AFRICA	11·3	23·3	7·9	8·5
North	12·8	23·9	2·7	2·9
Tropical and South	10·6	23·0	5·2	5·4
AMERICA	17·3	23·1	11·5	13·5
North	15·4	19·2	6·5	6·6
Middle	13·3	29·4	1·6	2·2
South	23·0	26·1	3·4	4·7
ASIA	11·0	21·1	53·3	56·1
South-West	9·3	28·3	2·4	2·6
South-Central	11·0	18·4	18·0	18·7
South-East	16·4	22·3	6·0	7·1
East	9·9	22·1	26·9	27·7
EUROPE	8·2	8·1	18·1	14·2
Northern and Western	6·1	6·8	6·3	4·7
Central	7·1	8·6	6·2	4·6
Southern	11·8	9·0	5·6	4·9
OCEANIA	18·2	26·9	0·5	0·5
U.S.S.R.	11·4	18·2	8·7	7·1

(Source: U.N., *Demographic Yearbook*, 1961.)

Types of Population Growth

It has often been suggested that there are a number of distinct stages in demographic growth through which populations pass, the stages being collectively known as the population cycle or demographic transition. The stages are drawn from European experience, but it does not follow that other populations will pursue the same course. Indeed, it is most likely that the experience of populations in non-industrial countries will be greatly telescoped through the benefit of technical assistance from the more advanced countries (Fig. 23). In other words, there is no rigid model of population growth,

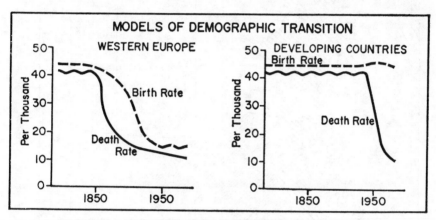

FIG. 23. Models of demographic transition, contrasting the developed and developing countries.

and the model for developing countries differs from that for developed countries. Consequently, the following classification of stages of population growth, which has been commonly used for developed countries, is not generally suitable for developing countries:

1. *High stationary phase*, with high fertility and mortality and only slow growth or a stationary population;
2. *Early expanding phase*, with high fertility and declining mortality causing an increasing rate of growth;
3. *Late expanding phase*, with declining fertility and mortality, and rapid increase;
4. *Low stationary phase*, with low fertility and mortality causing a fairly stationary population;
5. *Declining phase*, resulting from the fall of fertility below mortality.

It is perhaps better to think of types of population growth rather than stages, as for example in the United Nations classification made in the late 1950s, and adapted in Fig. 24 to the late 1960s:

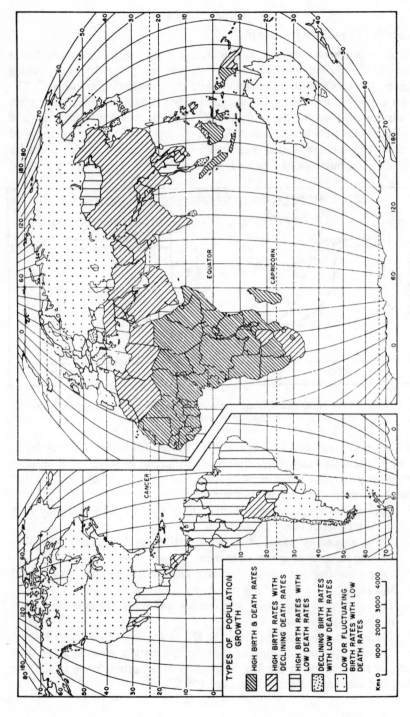

FIG. 24. Types of population growth in the 1960s.

1. *High birth and death rates*, common in some of the least-developed countries, as in tropical Africa;
2. *High birth rates and declining fairly high death rates*, as in many parts of South, South-East and East Asia;
3. *High birth rates and fairly low death rates*, common in tropical Latin America, where growth rates usually exceed 3 per cent per annum;
4. *Declining birth rates and low death rates*, as for example in Chile, Cuba, Ceylon and Malaysia;
5. *Low or fluctuating birth and death rates*, such as in most of Europe, North America and Japan.

The rapidity of population change in developing countries today gives a map such as Fig. 24 only short-term applicability.

Population Growth in Underdeveloped Countries

European populations have never grown at anything like the rate now pertaining in many underdeveloped countries. The peak of the natural increase of England and Wales was only 14 per thousand, and in Scandinavia it was 13. In many underdeveloped countries today it is over twice as large and, moreover, these countries are at a lower stage of economic development than Britain was at her peak of natural increase. The main reason is the dramatic reduction in mortality. In Mauritius, for example, the average life expectancy increased from 33 to 51 in an 8-year period after the Second World War, progress which Sweden took 130 years to achieve. And in Ceylon the campaign against malaria reduced the death rate from 22 to 10 per thousand in the period 1945 to 1952.

Most people are inclined to attribute the abrupt declines in mortality to modern medicine and public health measures, but some believe that economic progress is largely responsible, or that population growth has stimulated economic progress. However, there are few clear correlations between economic and demographic growth, and some of the highest rates of population growth (e.g. Latin America) are in areas which demonstrate no comparable economic advance. In fact, population growth seems to be delaying economic development (e.g. mechanization) and ensuring continued poverty. The gap between the rich and poor nations is growing.

The only large country outside the European tradition which has managed to pass through the same stages of demographic growth is Japan. An industrial nation, it has reacted in the same way as European countries faced with rapid population growth: it curtailed the growth for the benefit of all.

The rates of population increase are so high in the poor countries that there can be no quick economic solution. As Mountjoy states: "The whole problem of development, and particularly the furthering of industrialization, becomes more and more intractable with soaring population totals." In Java and Hong Kong and many other countries there is neither the space nor the time for slow demographic change. Even rich countries would find it extremely difficult to meet the challenge of doubling production with each generation. Economic progress is vital, but it must be accompanied by a reduction in demographic growth. Emigration is not a twentieth-century solution, except for small populations. In the long run, declining mortality would probably lead to a reduction in fertility, through the greater survival rate of children. Although difficult to prove or disprove, this has been proposed as an important cause for fertility decline in the West.

A more urgent solution is necessary, and this must surely be family limitation. It is not an easy solution. Many examples of failure of birth control propaganda, particularly in India, bear witness to this, but more and more countries are realizing the need for family limitation, and are implementing policies of fertility control, in an effort to induce social and economic change. Education will assist progress, as it encourages the desire for improvement in social standing, one of the principal causes of the reduction in fertility in advanced countries. In this situation the task of the industrialized countries is clear: they should do all in their power to help the poorer countries to achieve a more satisfactory balance between economic and demographic growth.

Local Population Changes

Geographers are more often concerned with local changes in population than with national change, and are interested in interpreting the complex patterns of population growth and decline and the relative significance of the two components: migration and natural change. In Chapter II it was noted how this is affected by the scale of the area analysed, migration being relatively more important in small areal units than in large ones.

Webb devised a useful Cartesian co-ordinate graph to plot natural and migrational components of population change, from which it is possible to derive eight types of change (Fig. 25):

A. Increase: natural gain exceeds net out-migration
B. Increase: natural gain exceeds net in-migration
C. Increase: net in-migration exceeds natural gain
D. Increase: net in-migration exceeds natural loss
E. Decrease: natural loss exceeds net in-migration
F. Decrease: natural loss exceeds net out-migration
G. Decrease: net out-migration exceeds natural loss
H. Decrease: net out-migration exceeds natural gain.

Modernization of a society leads to increased human mobility and greater areal variations in population numbers and characteristics. Age-structures vary more, and the range of natural increase/decrease is greater, as places with high fertility tend to have few deaths and places with high mortality tend to have few births. Old age-structures in advanced countries, especially in rural areas, are primarily responsible for the spread of natural decrease.

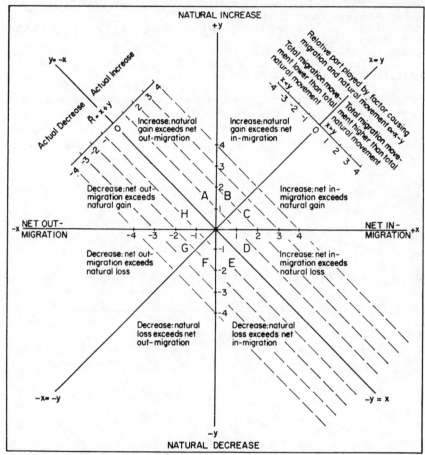

FIG. 25. Cartesian co-ordinate graph for showing types of population change (by kind permission of F. W. Carter).

References

BELSHAW, H., *Population Growth and Levels of Consumption*, 1956.

BOGUE, D., *Principles of Demography*, 1969.

BORRIE, W. D., *The Growth and Control of World Population*, 1970.

CLARK, C., *Population Growth and Land Use*, 1967.

CLARKE, J. I., *Population Geography and the Developing Countries*, 1971.

COALE, A. J. and HOOVER, E. M., *Population Growth and Economic Development in Low Income Countries*, Princeton, 1958.

COONTZ, S. E., *Population Theories and their Economic Interpretation*, 1957.

FREEDMAN, R. (ed.), *Population: The Vital Revolution*, New York, 1964.

162   *Population Geography*

HAUSER, P.M. (ed.), *The Population Dilemma,* Englewood Cliffs, 1963.
HAUSER, P. M. and DUNCAN, O. D., *The Study of Population,* Chicago, 1959.
MOUNTJOY, A. B., *Industrialization and Under-Developed Countries,* 1963.
MUDD, S. (ed.), *The Population Crisis and the Use of World Resources,* The Hague, 1964.
PETERSEN, W., *Population,* New York, 1961.
SAUVY, A., *General Theory of Population,* 1969.
SPENGLER, J. J. and DUNCAN, O. D. (eds.), *Population Theory and Policy. Selected Readings,* Glencoe, Ill., 1956.
STAMP, L. D., *Our Developing World,* 1960.
U.N., *The Future Growth of World Population,* 1958.
U.N., *1963 Report on the World Social Situation,* 1963.
VEYRET-VERNER, G., *Population: Mouvements, structures, répartition,* 1959.
WEBB, J. W., The natural and migrational components of population changes in England and Wales, 1921–31, *Econ. Geog.,* **39,** 130 (1963).

CHAPTER XI

POPULATION AND RESOURCES

CONSIDERATION of distribution or growth of population naturally poses questions of population numbers vis-à-vis resources. Are numbers too great or too small for the full utilization of the resources in a given area? What are the minimum, optimum and maximum numbers of people? When can the area be considered underpopulated or overpopulated?

Evaluations and Indices

Judgments of these questions are usually subjective and qualitative, and may be based on visual impressions. Resources are not easily measured quantitatively, and different populations have different needs, customs and ideals. In general terms, resources are substances or properties which satisfy human needs, and obviously they increase with the aims, talents and efforts of peoples, on their economic and cultural attainments and on their ability to exploit resources. Hence population/resource ratios are often highly subjective, and may be influenced by political and religious beliefs. Evaluations are generally related to the highest possible level of *per capita* income, but although economic criteria are instrumental, cultural factors should not be overlooked. There are no simple indices of optimum population, over-population or underpopulation. The U.N. volume *The Determinants and Consequences of Population Trends* examines the following eight, to which may also be added the dependency ratio:

1. *Per capita* income;
2. Level of employment;
3. Existence of diminishing returns;
4. Volume and direction of migration;
5. Changes of consumption patterns;
6. Life expectancy;
7. Changes in terms of international trade;
8. Measures of population density.

None are found wholly satisfactory, as all reflect other conditions apart from the relationship of population and resources, but some may be significant indices in specific cases.

The various concepts of overpopulation, underpopulation and optimum

163

population have no stable values in time and space. Optimum population in one region may be underpopulation or overpopulation in a similar region with people at a different economic and cultural level, and changing social and economic conditions mean that optimum population today may be over-population tomorrow. Population movements (natural and external) and technical advances are mainly responsible for this dynamic situation, but technical progress is not equally applicable in all parts of the world and does not everywhere produce the same results.

Optimum Population

Cantillon, the early-eighteenth-century mercantilist, was the first to consider the optimum size of population enabling the highest standard of living in a given area under given conditions. Superseding earlier ideas of the maximum population which could inhabit a given territory, he introduced the concept of the customs and traditions of the people as an important factor alongside that of the resources. The question posed is whether or not an increase in population will raise or lower the living standards of the inhabitants.

There is no doubt, for example, that under present social and economic conditions a total population of 10 millions in Britain would mean a decline in living standards, since many resources would become unusable and even the public services would have to be greatly reduced. On the other hand, 100 millions would require far greater resources than at present realized. Somewhere between lies the optimum. Where? Few writers have been bold enough to propose precise optima.

The economic optimum population, which has been defined as the number permitting the maximum *per capita* output in given technical and economic conditions, is the most usual connotation, but separate optima can be proposed for military power and social welfare. Indeed, the concept of optimum population has a political flavour as it is often considered only at national level, although it would be a very difficult matter to map the states with optimum populations.

Indications of an optimum population may be high average living standards, full employment, rational development of increasing resources and balanced demographic structure, but these are not precise criteria. Optima vary in time and space according to a wide variety of factors: the size of a state, its geography, social structure, stage of technical progress, quality of communications, etc. In general, the numerical range of the optimum is greater in varied economies and open environments than in specialized economies and isolated communities, where population growth, economic crises, war or drought may prove disastrous to the delicate balance between population and resources. Optima have been nearly achieved in the countries of North-West Europe, but in some, like The Netherlands, overpopulation is at hand.

In Europe and the United States the concept of optimum population gained some popularity in the years between the two world wars, but it has been severely criticized on theoretical and practical grounds, especially by communist writers, who see it as a Malthusian individualistic theory. Some demographers have found that optima cannot be calculated for existing conditions. Some find economy and society too dynamic to permit calculation of a satisfactory optimum. Others feel that the actual size of a population does not matter, and that the whole topic has received far too much attention.

Overpopulation

Overpopulation is said to occur when there is an excess of population over utilized or potential resources. It may result from an increase in population, a decline in resources, a decline in the demand for labour, or a combination of these factors. In other words, overpopulation may take place where resource development does not go hand in hand with population growth, and where growth of tertiary services lags behind technical progress.

Absolute overpopulation may be distinguished from relative overpopulation, the former occurring where the absolute limit of production has been attained though living standards remain low, while the latter indicates that present production is inadequate for the population although greater production is feasible. Relative overpopulation is more common than absolute overpopulation.

Overpopulation may be found at various levels: rural, industrial, regional, national. Rural overpopulation is common but is most striking in populous underdeveloped areas. In South-East Asia, where there is high fertility and declining mortality, intensive agriculture, land fragmentation and minimal mechanization, natural checks to overpopulation have exercised great control in the past. The demographic evolution of China has been frequently interrupted by famines, floods, droughts and epidemics. The *minifundia* of Malta and southern Italy, the crowding of fellaheen in the Nile delta, and the congested districts of western Ireland are similar in cause if not in character. Rural overpopulation may also result from (a) uneven distribution of lands between farmers, (b) increased mechanization and reduced demand for agricultural labourers, (c) a change from cultivation to livestock farming and again reduced demand for labour, and (d) rapid rural population growth. Many of these features can be seen in old countries of Europe. George sees famine, hunger, prolonged unemployment and increase of landless labourers and beggars as symptoms of rural overpopulation. Unfortunately, solutions other than emigration are slow and difficult, but in the long run social and cultural revolutions are more effective.

Industrial overpopulation is less obvious, because of the greater flexibility and mobility of labour in manufacturing compared with agriculture. It results either from technical progress causing redundancy of labour or of a product, or from the decline of a whole industry or group of industries. In Britain the textile industry offers many examples of the former, while shipbuilding is representative of the latter. Temporary or periodic declines associated with trade recessions or cycles cause temporary overpopulation; the world crisis of 1930 is a notorious example.

Where there is excessive reliance on a few basic industries, whole regions may be considered overpopulated; the "depressed areas" of inter-war Britain became great sources of internal and international migrants. In Belgium, Italy and Japan regional overpopulation is so common that it is a national problem. Even underpopulated countries like Australia, New Zealand and Brazil have their "islands" of overpopulation. Nowhere are discrepancies so marked as in Indonesia, where massive overpopulation in Java and some parts of Sumatra and Sulawesi (Celebes) contrasts vividly with underpopulation in Kalimantan (Borneo), the Lesser Sunda islands, the Moluccas and West Irian (New Guinea). Overpopulated islands, especially those with national status, are often faced with more serious problems than mainland countries; we think of Malta, Mauritius, Réunion, Hong Kong, Puerto Rico, Bermuda, Barbados and other West Indian islands. Some are lucky in having escape hatches to Britain or the United States.

Invariably overpopulation expresses itself only at the lowest levels of society: rural overpopulation affects the landless and the smallholders; industrial overpopulation hits the unskilled and semi-skilled workers. Communists see overpopulation as a feature of socially defective, unplanned capitalist societies. But will communist China ever be able to solve her inherited problem of overpopulation?

Maximum Population

Overpopulation is linked with the older concept of a maximum population above which the land cannot nourish any more without a decline in living standards and an increase in mortality. An absolute or true maximum population would seem unattainable in a modern economy, but may well be achieved in a primitive subsistence economy, especially where isolated, when birth rates and death rates are equal. No sound estimate of the absolute maximum world population is possible. In view of man's changing techniques and requirements, a relative or realized maximum is a more useful concept than an absolute maximum, as for instance in Italy and Ireland where it was relieved by massive emigration.

Underpopulation

Underpopulation may be said to exist where a population is too small to utilize fully its resources, or where the resources could support a larger population without lowering living standards or increasing unemployment. The former is more frequent than the latter.

Absolute underpopulation is quite rare, save in the case of isolated populations where numbers are incapable of normal demographic replacement or of adequate economic production. Relative underpopulation takes place where there is insufficient development of the resources available; nowhere is it more common than in the southern continents.

Underpopulation occurs among people with high living standards farming extensively; we find it in the Prairies and parts of Australia and New Zealand, partly as a result of the mode of settlement of near-virgin territory. Underpopulation may also occur at low technical levels, as among many pastoral nomads of arid regions and *chitemene* bush fallowers of the state of Zambia. In areas of advanced economy, it is difficult to rectify regional underpopulation, especially of rural areas, without government encouragement or colonization schemes. The break-up of *latifundia* in Italy and the agrarian reform measures in Egypt are both examples of government attempts to reduce local underpopulation. It is one of the claims of the socialist economies that regional inequalities are overcome. In backward societies, underpopulation may be resolved by improved medical facilities and diet and declining mortality.

Minimum Population

The minimum size of population becomes an interesting study in small isolated communities: in islands, mountain valleys, tropical forests, desert oases or Arctic wastes. Here the biological minimum may be distinguished from the economic minimum. Sauvy estimated the biological minimum for demographic replacement in a monogamous society to be 500 persons, enabling five marriages and 20 births per annum. In a polygamous group a slightly lower minimum is possible, but the dangers of disease and of adverse age-structures and sex-ratios are increased.

The economic minimum is more commonly found in advanced communities. It is the smallest number which permits division of labour within a group. Specialist occupations are no longer possible when numbers fall below this minimum, and outward migration takes place. In the Western Isles of Scotland the departure of young men and women often reduces numbers below the biological minimum; the departure of a doctor is often indictive that the economic minimum has been attained.

The World Situation

All the concepts mentioned in this chapter have been considered by numerous authors in relation to world population growth. An enormous literature has been devoted to discussions about the adequacy of resources to meet this growth. Differences of opinion result from different social and political ideals, as well as varied emphasis placed on the underlying influences upon population increase. Many writers, notably the Malthusians and neo-Malthusians, view with pessimism the prospects of an explosion of population which production will not satisfy. The fears are that death control is more widespread than birth control; that social organization in backward countries encourages population increase; that the world will be inundated by Asians; that the hundreds of millions who are hungry will augment; that standards of living will decline; that the gap between rich and poor nations will grow; that world food supplies will not match population growth. The vast negative areas (mountains, deserts, jungles, permafrost zones) are considered incapable of making an important contribution; the low-income countries of South-East Asia are considered too demographically fertile and too densely peopled to achieve high living standards in the immediate future.

Since the Second World War contrasting views have emerged concerning man's ability to meet the challenge of food supply, ranging from sublime optimism to imminent doom. Towards the end of the 1960s there was a noticeable movement towards guarded optimism, even among some formerly pessimistic Western experts, as a consequence of the early successes of the "green revolution". But there remain vast differences in opinion concerning the possibilities of extending the earth's cultivated area.

Other writers blame social institutions for the inconsistencies between population and resources. Some attack colonialism, some attack the class structure. Socialist and Marxist demographers stress the importance of social and economic revolutions as a means to reduce fertility and to raise living standards. They emphasize the technical feasibility of increased agricultural yields and industrial and energy production.

Ackerman has suggested a five-fold classification of the world into population/resource regions on the basis of population/resource ratios and the availability of technology (Fig. 26):

1. *United States type.* About one-sixth of the world's people live in technology–source areas with low population/resource ratios, as in much of North America, Australia and New Zealand and the U.S.S.R.

2. *European type.* One-sixth live in technology–source areas with high population/resource ratios, where industrialization and technology have permitted an expansion of resources through international trade. Most of Europe and Japan fall into this category.

3. *Egyptian type.* Roughly one-half live in areas which are technology-deficient with high population/resource ratios, as in India, Pakistan and China. Some of the most severe population problems are epitomized by this type.

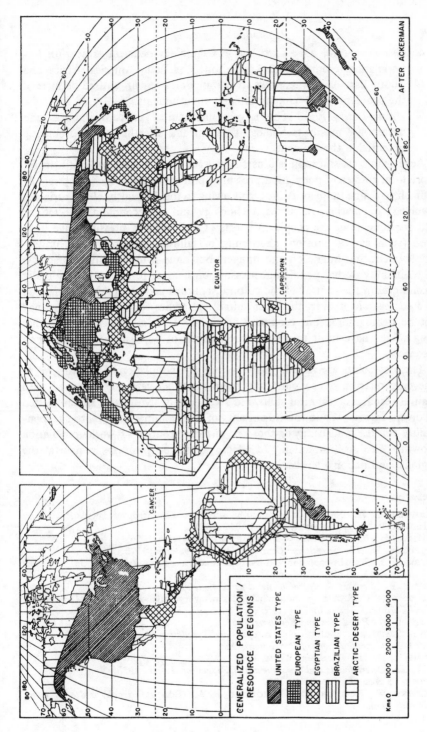

FIG. 26. Generalized population/resource regions (after E. A. Ackerman).

GENERALIZED POPULATION /
RESOURCE REGIONS

UNITED STATES TYPE

EUROPEAN TYPE

EGYPTIAN TYPE

BRAZILIAN TYPE

ARCTIC-DESERT TYPE

Kms 0   1000 2000 3000 4000

AFTER ACKERMAN

4. *Brazilian type.* One-sixth live in technology-deficient areas with low population/resource ratios, as in much of Latin America, Africa and South-East Asia, where resources sometimes remain unused because of the problems of developing difficult environments.

5. *Arctic–Desert type.* The largely uninhabited ice-caps, tundras and deserts are mostly technology-deficient and offer little food-producing potential at the moment.

Ackerman's classification is a useful general guide but offers little help for more local studies of population pressure upon resources, which is extremely difficult to define in quantitative terms owing to the dynamism of the variables involved: population, resources, technology and the economic expectations and attainments of the people. All sorts of indicators of pressure have been used (such as soil erosion, shortening of fallows, unemployment, under-employment, out-migration and hunger) but none is universally satisfactory. The difficulty is that population pressure on land or resources is only really meaningful in the context of the cultural, political and economic organization of a society. Moreover, the most suitable remedies for local pressures may not be demographic but economic or social. It is at this local level that geographers have most to offer in the analysis of population pressure upon resources.

The viewpoints are varied, partly because the population of the world is so unevenly distributed, so politically fragmented, so variously endowed with natural resources, technical skills and standards of living, and so committed to divers ideals. While the inhabitants of one country accept little responsibility for the well-being of those in another, control of world population growth seems an abstraction. In effect, population problems remain at the regional and national levels.

References

ACKERMAN, E. A., Population and natural resources, *The Study of Population*, ed. by HAUSER, P. M. and DUNCAN, O. D., p. 717 (1959).

BELSHAW, H., *Population Growth and Levels of Consumption*, 1956.

BORRIE, W. D., *The Growth and Control of World Population*, 1970.

CLARKE, J. I., World population and food resources: a critique, *Inst. Brit. Geogr. Special Volume*, no. **1**, 53 (1968).

GEORGE, P., *Questions de géographie de la population*, 1959.

KAMERSCHEN, D. R., On an operational index of overpopulation, *Economic Development and Cultural Change*, **13**, 169 (1965).

P.E.P., *World Population and Resources*, 1955.

ROYAL STATISTICAL SOCIETY, *Food Supplies and Population Growth*, 1963.

SAUVY, A., *General Theory of Population*, 1968.

STAMP, L. D., *Our Developing World*, 1960.

U.N., *The Determinants and Consequences of Population Trends*, 1953.

VEYRET-VERNER, G., *Population*, 1959.

ZELINSKY, W., KOSINSKI, L. and PROTHERO, R. M. (Eds.), *Geography and a Crowding World*, 1970.

INDEX